No Mess, No Message

Finding Strength in Struggle and Purpose in Pain

July 2020

Ashley —
Always be brave
to show your sparkle!

xoxo —
April

Dr. April Jones

Copyright © 2019 April Jones

Drifted Drum Company, LLC

www.thedrifteddrum.com
thedrifteddrum@gmail.com

ISBN: 978-1-7332147-0-4 (print)
ISBN: 978-1-7332147-1-1 (ebook)
ISBN: 978-1-7332147-2-8 (audiobook)

Ordering Information: Special discounts are available on quantity purchases by corporations, associations, and others. For details, contact us via our contact page at www.thedrifteddrum.com.

Scripture quotations from The Authorized (King James) Version. Rights in the Authorized Version in the United Kingdom are vested in the Crown. Reproduced by permission of the Crown's patentee, Cambridge University Press

Disclaimer:

The events described in this book are actual events but are represented as a reflection of my recollection and may contain inaccuracies due to skewed or biased perception or miscommunication. This book is not meant to shine negative light on any parties involved mentioned or not mentioned in this account. Also, this book is meant to encourage others but not intended to replace medical treatment—please seek help if needed. As a pharmacist, I fully support and encourage professional medical care. I am not a theologist. My views and interpretations of the Bible and faith are my own based on my knowledge, experiences, and personal spiritual relationship and are not necessarily the direct views or opinions of the churches and educational institutions I have been affiliated with. I cannot claim any liability for any changes in feelings or actions based on others' changes in perceptions as a result of reading this book; people are responsible for their own actions and opinions.

Special Thanks

I need to first thank my husband, Billy, for being my rock, my realist, and my supporter and for always loving me more than I love myself. I am so, so thankful for my three boys. Nothing brings me more joy than being your mom.

I want to give special thanks to my family and friends for being part of my story and allowing me to share the good, the bad, and the ugly that has painted the picture of my life. I am so grateful to my friends who have been my sounding board for this book, encouraging me, reading my drafts, giving me meaningful feedback, and reminding me of the purpose of telling this story.

I want to commemorate Madelyn Beamon, Wesley McCall, Vivian "Abbi" Shaw, and Shae Pierce. Their lives were taken from this Earth before anyone here was ready to lose them. Their parents, especially their moms, have been a daily inspiration to me the last 15 years.

I also write this in honor of my friends in heaven, Danielle Beith, likely the most resilient yet humble and kind person I've ever met, and Julia Fuller, who was the kind of friend you never forget your whole life. She was a perfect example of what being a Christian should look like—warm, beautiful, and funny. I literally miss you every day, Julia, especially your laugh.

I have been privileged to meet many strong, amazing people, heroes in their own rights. People who battled like warriors, people who lost the most precious people in their life, yet who continue to smile. They continue to touch the lives of others. They are genuine. They are complex. They are generous. They are awesome.

To all these people who have taught me so much just by being the best version of yourselves, I thank you.

I give thanks to my Lord and Savior, Jesus Christ, and am grateful, truly grateful, for every day and every opportunity to smile at the world. It's my goal to spread my newfound sense of gratitude, compassion, and confidence to others.

Contents

As you build your walkway of strength, pave with positivity and grout with grit. Then be sure to show others the path of resilience through the struggle you took so much care to make.

—Me

This Is About You

BEGINNING THE JOURNEY
TO NEW PERSPECTIVE

There is a well-known phrase: "If at first you don't succeed, try and try again." Yet the definition of insanity is to do the same thing over and over, each time expecting different results.

So, how are we supposed to make sense of this advice?

They also say history repeats itself. The only logic I can find to tie these together is that history only repeats itself if we don't learn from our mistakes, and if we do intend to try and try again, we'll be risking insanity if we don't change the approach.

That is not going to fit on a coffee mug.

A book about resilience, overcoming adversity, and finding humble gratitude is not for everyone. But this book might be for you if:

- You have ever been through or are going through something in your life that you feel is earth-shaking, mind-blowing, utterly unfair, and incomprehensible.

- You have experienced a painful event that was caused by someone else, by your own doing, by supernatural events, or by plain bad luck.

- You feel like bad things should not happen to good people.

- You feel like you are a bad person because of things you have done to yourself or others, and there is no way to come back from it.

- You feel desperate, like the light at the end of your tunnel is a train, or you feel like optimism is for losers.

I want you to learn from my journey.

I want you to be able to cope with your pain and struggles in an empowered way.

You can't control what happens, but you can control how you see it and how you respond.

This, my friend, has been the key that has opened my heart to happiness I didn't know existed: finding faith, gaining grit (defined as courage and resolve; strength of character), and a grateful heart.

April Dawn Jones, BS, PharmD, MBA, but some people just call me Sunshine.

This is my story. These are my struggles, my emotions, and this is what I've learned along the way, but this book is not about me. Not really. It is about my desire to share these things with you because I don't want a minute of what I have experienced to be wasted.

You gain strength, courage, and confidence by every experience in which you really stop to look fear in the face. You must do the thing which you think you cannot do.

—Eleanor Roosevelt

I suppose I should start by saying hello.

Hi! My name is April. It's really nice to meet you!

On the outside I may seem to have it all together. I have been married for almost 20 years to my high school sweetheart. We have three active, precious boys ranging in age from seven to 17, each with unique talents and interests. I also enjoy a successful career as a medical director in oncology. I have several letters behind my name. I am seen by most as a positive person.

But I, like many, didn't have an easy path. I have had to work hard, and things didn't always go as planned, as you will see. I became a mom at an early age, and my first son was diagnosed with cancer and endured an amputation when he was only two years old. The journey of becoming a woman, a functional adult, a mom; finding my faith; realizing my goals, and still being everything I needed to be to everyone who needed me was not an easy one.

But I didn't let the pressures of unfortunate circumstances crush me. I was damaged, yes, but I have learned so much in the flames. And to me, all of that was wasted if I don't share these things with you.

I am not spectacular. My story is no more sad or special than any other story.

I have, however, made certain I learn something from every challenge, every disappointment, every struggle.

I have grown to believe if I make just one person know the part they play is essential and that they have the potential to impact every other person they touch, then drive, compassion, and kindness can become contagious.

This is my approach for every aspect of my life.

I haven't always been this way.

It was in the struggle where I gained strength. It was the purpose I found in the pain that changed my views. It was redemption through Christ and developing a relationship with God that renewed me.

It has been a process of breaking and rebuilding, mistakes, regret, forgiveness, grinding and polishing to reveal the potential underneath. I learned it is essential to find courage to push yourself to do more than you think you can, to take each challenge in pieces, and build on the small successes until you realize your dream, the dream that everyone has— to be joyful and content in life and with who you are. To appreciate your imperfections and improvements, and strive to continue to be a better version of yourself. I learned the importance of seeking God's plan for my life and aligning my actions with his will.

As you read about my journey, you will understand why I have a **free spirit** and a **grateful heart**, and why I love my life, the only one I get. I hope that you will find your ability to do just the same. I hope that you find hope and faith in these pages.

Introducing...Me

THE IMPORTANCE OF KNOWING WHERE YOU CAME FROM

It's not what others think of you that define you: it's who Christ says you are, who you know yourself to be, who you believe you can become, and your willingness to follow Christ's will for your life that will determine your success.

But there is value in recognizing where you came from. It will help you to fully appreciate who you are, where you are now, where you are going, and God's plan for you.

Whether you are proud of where you came from, ashamed of it, or pretend it doesn't matter, you either let where you came from propel you forward or hold you back. But the good thing is, you get to choose.

Only God Almighty has been named the Alpha and the Omega, the beginning and the end.

The rest of us—every plant, insect, animal, and human—well, we all had to start somewhere, and if we are going to tell our story, why not start there, at the beginning? Here's mine.

Cue the backdrop.

Small Town, America. Not a small town near the beach where you could go on adventures to find sea shells after school. Not a small town in the mountains where you and your friends would ride bikes to the creek to throw rocks. Small Town, West Tennessee.

In the middle of never-ending flat fields, there were modest houses and small schools, a tiny grocery store, a vintage-esque post office, a gas station that sold suckers that tasted like SweeTarts and only cost a dime. The speed limit was 25 mph (and still is), and no one actually drove that fast. All the kids rode bikes in the street.

Everybody knew everybody else, and nobody locked their doors. It wasn't uncommon for kids to roost on somebody's porch for the day in the summer or congregate at the playground at school until it got dark or they heard their mom yelling for them to come eat.

We rode four-wheelers in cotton fields and across yards and never wore helmets. We weren't strangers to getting a burn from riding a few too many kids at one time and grazing a leg on the hot parts under the seat.

We caught fireflies in Mason jars and played kickball in the empty lot beside the school. We used our manners and respected the property of others. Grown-ups were mostly kind and tolerant of the neighbor kids.

This was the backdrop of my life. This was small-town life in the '80s and early '90s with girls and boys that I will remember forever. No matter how far away our lives took us or how different or distant we have become, this is where I grew up.

The biggest vacation adventure I can remember was going to Chicago to see my cousins. The houses were closer together and we played in the sprinklers across the row of yards with the neighbor kids. We rode our bikes in the alley and walked with the grown-ups to the Italian ice stand.

It seemed like outside their street, the world was busy, bustling, and exciting. Before this, I thought every town was just like mine but theirs was a definite contrast to the miles and miles of farmland I knew.

Intro: The Family

When I turned seven, I became a big sister. I prayed to have a sister, and I did. She had dark curly hair and cute chubby cheeks and followed me every-where. I was her protector, even when she was bossy or whiny. She was my favorite person in the world, and still today she is the Thelma to my Louise (minus the final scene, I suppose).

My dad worked as a mechanic when I was little. I remember him working on his own projects in our garage. Then he went to night school, got his own business, and worked a lot more. My mom was an artist but mainly she stayed home with me and my sister.

I didn't know it then, but I was pretty blessed.

Life was simple. Things were simple. I didn't think we were rich but if we were poor, I didn't know it. My mom was frugal, but we had food and a house and a car and we had pizza on Fridays, so life was good.

Why can't we freeze that feeling?

That feeling of simplicity and safety. The feeling of freedom and contentment. Why can't we keep it around us like a mosquito net blocking out the fears and threats of the world that try to suck the life out of our veins?

Exposing ourselves to the realities of complex life, difficult relationships, unexpected troubles, and unintended consequences can shake our confidence if we are not grounded in God's promises.

In a small town, who you know is likely everybody around you!

If you start to think that the only way you can amount to anything is if the people in your immediate realm like you or believe in you, then you are on pretty shaky ground.

You know that saying, "It's not what you know, it's who you know that matters?"

Well, I think that is a really crappy thing to say for the most part. When referring to the Lord Almighty, maybe I'll agree with you, and I can definitely vouch that there are opportunities that have come my way by divine introduction to the right person at the right time.

But if you think that is the only way you can get anywhere, it lends power to a pretty dismal outlook.

Realize this: wherever you are, whatever your skills are or dreams, know that other people will *not* dictate your destiny.

You can stay right where you are and grow right where you are planted, or you can pioneer past the horizon, but you finding yourself starts inside you. You don't need any other person to make you into something great or get you where you want to be.

We can be a willing vessel. We can offer God our heart and eager hands. Pray for him to show us His will and plans for our life. He intends for His people to be blessed. We are not promised a life free of adversity, but the *Bible* says that He has plans for prosperity and a future for His people.

My high school, with its graduating class of a hundred kids, was the only one in the whole county, a county that didn't even have one stoplight.

This is where I started.

This place filled with more corn and cotton fields than neighborhoods or places to go. This place where our main entertainment was sittin' on the courthouse square or riding backroads.

This is where I learned to love music and read books. This is where I fell in love, just like it says in a country song, with a blue-eyed boy, when I was only 16 years old.

But, this is *not* where I found out who I am.

By tenth grade that small town began to feel more and more like a pillow trying to smother me. The fields that lay beyond the town felt like they were never ending, like there was nothing beyond them, like I was on a raft in the very middle of the ocean with no clue which way to the closest shore.

Life for me would change.

After my parents divorced and my sense of trust and security and innocence had vanished, I struggled to find ways to fill the empty space inside me. Most of these were unsuccessful. I would eventually leave that town.

Maybe I was loved and maybe I was in a safe place but those things did not fill that space. I viewed love and safety as fleeting and dependent on circumstance. People can always choose to leave. I didn't know that what I needed was a personal relationship with God—love and safety that was unconditional.

I wanted more out of this life than what I saw around me. My soul was not content and I didn't know why. I wanted to do something important. I wanted to change the world. I wanted to find out what my talents were and see what I could be capable of. And while I dreamed of what life could be like outside this town and wondered what my future might hold, I didn't know that I wasn't so alone in those desires.

Every night in every town everywhere, there is a teenage girl who looks out her window at the stars and wishes her life could be magical, romantic, and fulfilling. She wishes she will be successful and admired. She wishes for everything to be easy.

But for most, things in life don't come easy. I learned fairytales have scary parts but mostly they also have happy endings.

So yes, I found my prince early, when he noticed me across the gas station parking lot. Me and my friend Angela stopped to fill up before she drove me home from a night spent hanging out. He was talking to a pretty blonde then. When he saw me, he stopped midsentence and held his hand up. I assumed he asked the girl if she knew who I was because she looked over too. I laughed, blushed, and got in the car.

From that moment on, our paths could not uncross. We officially met at a football game a couple of weeks later and the rest is history. We were pretty much inseparable after that day.

I was the academic, and he was the athlete. I like a good party and loud music, he became a police officer and abhors a crowded scene. I love to dance, he'd rather not.

But the rest, *the stuff that really matters, that's where we came together*, and knowing I wouldn't be alone when I left this town gave me the courage to actually do it.

Spoiler alert: but if life for us was going to be all sunshine and roses, you wouldn't be reading this book.

I wish I could say there is something you can do to stop time when everything is good and just replay it. I wish we could know when the conflicts in our story are coming and fast forward through those parts.

But we can't do that. We can, however, remember that even when you feel ugly, tainted, boring, unworthy, weak, or even broken, it takes a lot of nearly unbearable heat and pressure to make a diamond, one of the strongest and most beautiful stones created. Before all of that, that lump of ashy carbon may have seemed pretty ordinary, **but the potential was there all along.**

> *"Character cannot be developed in ease and quiet. Only through experience of trial and suffering can the soul be strengthened, ambition inspired, and success achieved."*

> —Helen Keller

The Blame Game

WHO CAN WE POINT AT WHEN BAD THINGS HAPPEN?

People question why bad things happen to good people, but truthfully bad things happen to all people. Sometimes there is nowhere to place the blame.

If bad things happen to everyone, then it is vital to feel them and face them so you can be strong to fight another day.

When something bad happens, we ask ourselves, "Why is this happening to me?" We ask, "What did I do to bring this on?", "Is God mad at me?", and a ton of other illogical questions to try to explain the why and begin to cope.

When we are angry, we need something or somebody to direct our anger towards. But cancer is not tangible. I can yell, and it won't hear me. I can throw something, and it won't hurt cancer like cancer hurts those it clings to.

So instead, we turn the blame inwards.

I was 22 years old, and I thought I was in control. I was confident the world would be whatever I made it if I just put in hard work and smart planning. But I wasn't prepared for the circumstances I now faced. I had a baby with cancer.

Rewind

Two years before this, I was alone in my bedroom on a Saturday night. I was up late reading a book. I had a weird feeling, quite possibly my first-ever anxiety attack. I felt nauseous and nervous at an unusual thought: "Maybe I am…*pregnant.*"

I had little reason to think this. I was three weeks past my twentieth birthday and 12 weeks into marriage. My husband and I were living almost two hours apart due to work and school. It was a planned but temporary living arrangement. I'd seen Billy maybe twice in the last month. I was on birth control and we were more than careful.

I was young, with big ambitions and a focused route.

When I turned 17, I wanted to be on the fast track to success. Sure, I was engaged already, but love was not enough for me to be happy. I was on a mission to build a bigger and shinier life than the one I knew. With only half a credit left to graduate in the middle of my twelfth-grade year, I made a plea to the principal and school board that was granted, and I started attending college full time. I was taking 18 credit hours that semester as my peers had fun sliding through the home stretch to graduation.

I scheduled large class loads every term and took courses in the summer. As a double major in chemistry and biology, I was set to complete it all in only three years, and I got a job at the hospital in the lab so I could not just learn more but also be in an environment that would keep my goals in front of me.

I loved Billy and he gave me no reason to think he would ever abandon me, but I wanted to know that if he ever left me to fend for myself that I could be completely independent. Leaning on others felt unsafe. I was driven to build a future that would provide for me (and us as a couple).

In addition to that, I wanted to help people. I thought that the medical field, drug development, and oncology research would be the perfect place for me to do that and to challenge myself. I liked challenge. I liked learning. My eyes were on the prize, and I understood that it would take hard work to get there. I was prepared for that.

College was a profound time for me. I was having the time of my life but not in the way that many enjoy the college life. No parties or drinking. I was focused on my mission. For the first time, I felt genuinely happy in my own skin. I was independent. I had some true close friends. I sang in choir and was in the chemistry society. I was in this storybook relationship. I felt smart and in control.

It was such a change from the insecurities I had experienced for most of my life. I didn't want anything to change.

Pregnancy at this stage in the game meant I would be irreversibly stuck, which is what urged me to plead to the guy upstairs. I didn't think much about premonition. Yet there I was praying, "Lord, *please* don't let me be pregnant, but if I am, please just make it go away!"

Cue the gasps, followed by frowning faces and your temptation to put this book down right now, but stay with me. It makes me feel horrible, even now, to think about how naïve and selfish and young I was, and I am truly appalled at the thought.

I had no idea what it meant to be a parent.

There are many women who are unable to have babies, and there are other reasons why I am ashamed to think back on this moment in my life, but truthfully, right then, there was nothing I wanted less than a baby.

You *have* to be kidding!

Six hours later I was at work. I worked part time as a clerk and phlebotomist in the lab at the hospital. We were bored. It was a quiet Sunday morning before orders were due to come in and there wasn't much happening in the emergency room either.

One of the supervisors encouraged us to get some training in to break up the silence. She wanted to teach me how to process pregnancy tests. Since it was slow and we had no patient samples, she told me to, well you know…pee in a cup.

Despite the prior night's eerie feelings, I pushed back, "That will be a waste of time! I know mine will be negative," I said. "I won't even know if I work the machine wrong because it will show nothing either way!"

"Then what's the big deal? It's just for learning, anyway," she said.

So, I peed. As we waited the allotted time for the results, we chatted mainly about school.

"What would you do if you *are* pregnant?" She asked.

I started talking about how Billy and I might be newlyweds, but we'd been together for over three years. I told her we planned to have kids one day, so if it happened now it wouldn't be the end of the world.

Blah, blah, blah, so on and so on. This was my superficial answer because it seemed to be the most appropriate one to this question. It was believable and was how I thought I should feel, but it was not how I felt. As the image of last night's anxiety flashed in my brain, I knew that giving her this answer because it was the logical response still did not make it true.

She stopped me and said, "No. April, really. What would you do if you *are* pregnant?"

Then she showed me my positive pregnancy test.

My initial reaction shocked me.

When I processed what she said, I freaked out! I put my hands on my cheeks. My face turned red, my heart started to race, and I began to cry. (I was not a crier. Well, in public, anyway.) She told me to hurry to the bathroom and take a minute to process, calm myself, and "make the call" (to tell The Dad, of course).

I was in the bathroom for about 15 minutes. I cried uncontrollably for the first 10. Then I washed my face and waited for the redness to fade a little before emerging.

I picked up the phone and dialed Billy. He was on patrol that morning. After he said hello, my words just spilled out, barely discernible between my sobs. (They were coming again.)

I was so upset!

He was so angry.

The conversation ended pretty quickly.

Billy was angry not that I was pregnant but because I was *sad* about being pregnant.

After all that time together and now that we were married, he was elated that I was having his baby, and I was sad! I began to feel my stomach turn with guilt. I had ruined his moment. This very special moment that he finds out he is going to be a father for the first time, and **I ruined it with tears, fear, and disappointment.** I could never take that back or redo that, and *I ruined it with my selfishness.* I still feel regret about this.

My college bestie, Sarah, worked at the hospital too, and she was scheduled to come in for her shift at any minute. I knew she would help me sort out my feelings and make a plan to work this new baby into my life.

It was only about 7:30 a.m., and it was still slow at work. I had to get a handle on things before orders started coming in. After all, I had to make it through my shift, and I was not going to let a little thing like pregnancy slow me down!

After a few tears and hugs the second she came in, Sarah and I started counting weeks and talking through logistics. We determined the baby would be due during winter break. I'd have a full four to five weeks off after his due date, then I could be back at it without missing a day of class. I started to feel a little better about this "situation."

So next I just needed to apologize to Billy, tell him how "excited" I was, that everything would be ok, that things were still on track, and...oh, I had to figure out how to tell my mom.

Trying to make the most of it.

Okay, so it wasn't exactly like an episode of MTV's *16 and Pregnant*, but if there were a college edition, I could have starred in it.

And while you already know how the first few minutes of discovery went, the next seven months weren't quite as dramatic, but I did feel like an alien in my own body.

I went to a small Christian college, and I worked hard to get there on a scholarship. I had plans to be more and do more than "just a mom." At the time, I saw it as settling. Although I was married, three whole months to be exact, I was embarrassed and felt out of place at school as a mom-to-be. I had wanted to make an impact on the world. I wanted to build a different kind of life than the one I grew up in.

I did not want to get married to be a homemaker with what I pictured as a quaint little life. To me, being married meant having a partner to support me on this adventure I was embarking on. I did not want to change those plans. I did not want to sacrifice my ambitions. My plan indicated medical school or pharmacy school as my next step, so the kids around me were driven, too. They were not married. They were not pregnant.

I spent all of high school trying so hard to fit in. In college, I finally did, and then I had to go and make myself an outcast, *again*!

But I had found my tribe. I was amidst the funniest, smartest, most caring people I had ever met, and they still embraced this new, more "round" version of me. My newfound friends didn't treat me differently. They encouraged me and were considerate. They tried to make me feel like this experience and I were very special.

But I felt different.

My teachers were kind and the other students didn't seem to make a fuss over my big belly when it started to show. But I felt like I stuck out like a sore thumb. I wondered if they all were judging me, thinking:

"She had so much potential."

"Wow, how careless!"

"I hope she finishes."

The funny thing is in that small town where I grew up, not 30 minutes from those very halls, many girls had babies right out of high school, sometimes even while they were in high school. So, what was different?

Only one thing: my perspective.

These sweet, supportive people were not judging me. **It was all me!** I was thinking all those things. I was judging myself. I was harsh on myself because my surroundings had changed, and I had a new standard to measure myself by. And although my surroundings were positive and accepting, I had self-doubt. **I felt like my circumstances were out of my control,** and I had only my plan on the drawing board. I was not giving any consideration to the idea God may have had a different plan altogether.

My happiness and success in college helped me redefine and mold the person I believed I was capable of being. I was starting to really feel good about being me. So, when I was barely blossoming into this capable confident person, growing another little person, for whom I was going to have to be responsible, shook my new world like an earthquake.

I *thought* that if I was a good person, a person who had asked for redemption from my sin and avoided a sinful lifestyle, that it must be in God's will. I *thought* that being in a Christian environment and conforming to those values was enough.

Despite my upbringing and immersion in a religious atmosphere, I still didn't recognize that having a personal relationship with God was more than just those things. I had no idea that being the best me I could be did not equate to fulfilling God's will, and that making my own plans without seeking direction from God might mean a path that was completely misaligned with his intended one. I thought he would just be okay with whatever I decided and support me in that.

I wondered if the pregnancy could somehow be God's punishment for youthful sin or being proud and ambitious. This was not my plan, and if I was not simply being punished, and this was indeed God's plan, then *why*?

It wasn't easy.

For the majority of the pregnancy, Billy and I weren't living together aside from summer break. His police department near Memphis was almost two hours from where I went to school and still lived with my parents. Eventually, we thought, I'd join him, and attend one of the great pharmacy or medical schools there.

But the separation was still hard, and living at home with my mom emphasized my unreadiness to have a baby.

It was a happy peaceful place, but I felt like a butterfly with one wing still stuck in a cocoon. I was so lucky to have my family with me, and I now know they helped me more than I realized: laundry, dinner, buying groceries—but it all meant I didn't feel like a grown-up mom, not yet.

In my bedroom, I put a crib next to the full-size, white-and-gold banister bed I had slept in every night since kindergarten. I still slept across the hall from my little sister. I had a small desk under my window, passed down from my step-grandpa, where I did homework under a wallpaper border with books printed on it. But in this home, I was not the mom. I was the daughter.

Things were not as I planned.

It was surreal to hear the heartbeat at my ultrasounds. Billy went to *every* single appointment with me. He was young too, but his excitement helped me feel happy this was happening to me—like it or not, I believed I could do this in an "I am so tired, but I can do anything" kind of way.

But it was the kicking inside my belly that really made me fall in love with Tyler.

At first, I didn't know they were kicks. With all the heartburn, I probably thought they were little gas bubbles, but the doctor told me they were kicks. I think every minute of every day after that, I actively anticipated them.

The kicks made him really real.

These kicks on the inside reminded me that what was growing was more important than any judgment (mine or anyone else's), more than circumstance. Tyler was more important than the fact that I didn't have a nursery (he would end up sleeping with me anyway), more important than how old I was or how ready I was or how much I knew about being a mom. I would love him more than anything else in my life when he came, more than I loved myself.

It's really good I got on board because **I had no idea about the storms to come.**

During the pregnancy, I still behaved in many ways like a typical college student. Looking back, I realize how much my young subconscious was still in denial.

When you are 20, you can do a lot of things. You can vote, you can buy a car, get married, rent an apartment. You can't buy alcohol in the US, but you can make life-changing decisions and get pregnant (purposefully or accidently). Being 20 also means there are many opportunities for maturity still, but of course I was completely blind to them then. I still had trouble weighing the risks and benefits of all of my actions accurately.

I hung out with my friends when I needed a laugh, I blasted music when I was moody, I sunbathed in my bikini, big belly and all, with my best friends. I took afternoon naps like a cat in the sunroom, and I ate whatever and whenever I wanted without understanding or pausing to consider the possible consequences. That included a lot of Chinese food, Wendy's Frosties with fries, and chips and queso. If a big test was coming, I'd eat chocolate chip pancakes for breakfast at IHOP. I gained 65 pounds so fast. I was oblivious, and my pregnant belly didn't feel so pretty. I was accustomed to being a healthy weight pre-pregnancy. Getting fat was something I never worried about before. I could eat chocolate ice cream with chocolate syrup and chocolate chips for breakfast and never gain a pound before, and I did! Being fit had been a product of good metabolism and a very active lifestyle that negated most of my bad eating habits. The quick weight gain now made a nice little layer of fat appear right below my nice round belly as my body protested my abuse.

And so ensued Storm Number One.

It was a chilly November day, and I gave my research project presentation to a room full of chemistry and biology students that morning. I was hot. Not the good kind of hot but the red-faced sweaty kind of hot. And my head was throbbing.

Afterwards, I made the 90-minute drive to a routine checkup at my OB-GYN as soon as I finished up. Billy, as always, met me there. He was already shaping up to be a great dad—he was so excited about our little champ. But at the checkup, my blood pressure was a shocking 180/120, and I was admitted to the hospital immediately.

Now, I have not researched causes of preeclampsia thoroughly but from most of what I have read, there has not been a specific definitive cause pinpointed. There is, however, speculation by many sources that there is possibly a relationship between genetics, insufficient blood flow to the uterus, poor nutrition, and a high percentage of body fat and preeclampsia.

My doctor was old school in his views on women. He told me I shouldn't be in school worrying about making a career. I should be at home worrying about becoming a mom and taking care of my baby. We didn't see eye-to-eye on that. He also suggested that my poor diet, with all the salt and sugar, could be the cause of this onset of illness.

"For Pete's sake, I take my vitamins literally every day, isn't that sacrifice enough?!" I thought. Obviously, my heavy coursework of chemistry and biology had not yet covered healthy lifestyle, obstetrics, or nutrition yet, but even if it had, I still had that youthful feeling of invincibility that clouded my judgment and underlying denial still was rooted stubborn like a weed.

I felt like a failure, and Tyler wasn't even here yet.

I thought about all the other things I had put my body through while pregnant. Not alcohol, drugs, or cigarettes but I was around chemicals in the lab at school all day. Were those bad, too?

I realized maybe penciling this baby in on my schedule wasn't enough. And if I thought getting pregnant might throw a kink in things, Tyler's birth also did not go as I had planned.

I was in the hospital for an entire week while they pumped me with fluids and diuretics and gave me steroids for his lungs. I blew up like a balloon, and I'm not exaggerating!

If Eddie Murphy had happened to be in Memphis visiting a relative in the hospital and saw me in the hall, he would have immediately paid me millions to star in footage for a new *Nutty Professor* movie, perhaps calling it *Nutty Chemistry Student*. I was unrecognizable. I could barely see out of my eyes because my face was so swollen, and even my knitted Old Navy house shoes would not fit over my feet. I felt like if somebody touched my skin it would burst open like that turkey on the table on National Lampoon's *Christmas Vacation*.

I stuck it out as long as I could but on the following Friday at 8 p.m., the chief physician came in and said, "We are not waiting anymore. Let's just do this."

Of course, this was the only two-hour window during which Billy felt confident nothing exciting or important would happen. He had run back to the apartment to take a quick shower and grab us a couple of movies. I called him frantically, and I can't imagine how fast he must've driven to get back because he was scrubbing up in plenty of time.

Little but fierce.

Tyler entered the world via C-section seven weeks early. He weighed 3 pounds, 14 ounces, and he was fuzzy like a little duck. We may not have known how to be parents to this tiny fragile thing, but we knew we loved him even before we saw him.

I prayed for him to be healthy and strong and come home soon, and even though I was only 33 weeks along, without the ventilator he breathed all on his own! He started drinking from a bottle the very next day and spent only a week in the neonatal intensive care unit before being discharged!

My blood pressure was still elevated when he came home, and my body was a mess. Every drop of cocoa butter I had used the last few months was wasted, since the fluid they pumped into me had left me with so many stretch marks I felt like a zebra, and my stomach, which I still feel so insecure about (Billy affectionately refers to it as a comfortable condo for his three off-spring) was unrecognizable, but that's *just* skin…right?

Tyler though, *he* had overcome the danger and far exceeded anybody's expectations in his very first week of life. He came out a fighter.

I thought our worst was behind us.

I felt blessed to get through such a scary time. Little did I know, we were being conditioned for round two.

My semester wasn't over, but my teachers were gracious and my friends were so helpful. I was able to make up what I missed. It didn't go as planned, but we made it nonetheless.

I was crazy about Tyler!

I wasn't perfect. I was feeling bummed out about all the changes to my body and feeling isolated. For a few weeks, I coped mostly with frozen chocolate-covered graham crackers dipped in Cool Whip and episodes of *Allie McBeal*. Not the best decision, but I now realize I probably had a case of postpartum depression. With my lack of sleep and my body in disrepair, I spent all day alone with a new baby while Billy went to work and my friends at school were living "normal" lives. My identity and my confidence were slipping.

But as we settled in, Tyler became my sidekick. I took him everywhere with me, except class, and quit my part-time job at the hospital so I could spend all my extra time enjoying being a mommy.

I had no idea that life could get any better, but it had.

It was new and different, but I loved my new role and my little perfect guy.

So when we got the news that turned our world upside down, I remembered that prayer. Not the one for him to be healthy and strong and come home to spend every single moment with me but **the other one.**

I remember those big tears I cried when I found out I was expecting and how they weren't happy tears. I remembered that feeling of being sick at the thought of being pregnant and now I was sick at the thought of losing him. I was terrified that it was my fault because of that moment that I was naïve and selfish and didn't want him.

What I know now:

Our actions can be destructive and lead to consequences but merely **having a bad thought, a moment out of character, will not curse us.**

Focusing those resentful angry feelings on yourself for whatever reason you make up will not help strengthen you to cope with what is at hand, **and self-loathing will not make you feel better.**

What I didn't know then is that becoming a young mom would not be the end to my short story and being born a preemie and then getting a life-threatening diagnosis would not be the end to Tyler's.

Rock-a-Bye Baby

WHAT IT LOOKS LIKE
WHEN THE BOUGH BREAKS

Rational people try to reason through a situation.

Sometimes this is a very successful approach to coping. The problem with this is that childhood illness and most other traumatic life-altering events rarely have a transparent reason. **It is not rational, and you can't reason your way out of it**.

As parents we try to protect our children from the bad, but there are some things we can't control. **Some things are inevitable.** We can't avoid it. We only get to decide how we respond.

"Rock-a-Bye Baby," the lullaby, comes to mind. This sweet little baby is rock-in' in the breeze and *bam*. The bough breaks and down comes baby, cradle and all! (Really? Seriously? We sing this to our children!)

But that's how life is sometimes. We are happy and peaceful just chilling in the breeze until our bough breaks.

You may think that becoming a Christian means God should protect us from all adversity.

In John 10:10, the apostle John says, "The thief comes only to steal, and kill, and destroy; I came that they might have life, and might have it abundantly."

The battle of good and evil was in effect long before we were created. I believe that God does not bring troubles upon us, but the book of Job teaches us that God may in fact allow trials to afflict us.

In doing so, He tests our faith. We have the opportunity to grow, and we learn to lean on Him. It doesn't mean that He is not able or that He doesn't care enough to shield you or save you. But there are many examples in the *Bible* where God allows His people to be victimized. Many times, His people were persecuted for being Christians, but God's grace and victory still shine through, even if it's only realized through eternal life.

Peter was thrown in jail. Daniel was thrown into a den of lions. Shadrach, Meshach, and Abednego were put into a furnace! And of course, Jesus was crucified. Rather than saving them from these unfathomable events, God allowed the envelopes to be pushed. But in the end, angels freed Peter from his shackles and he walked out of jail, Daniel was found in the den untouched, those three Hebrew fellas were seen walking around in the fire with what appeared to be a fourth man, and Jesus rose from his tomb on the third day! Even death could not overcome God's will and purpose.

We can hold onto hope.

So, let's pause a minute.

You may still be wondering how I got to this point. What was it like juggling being a new mom, grad school, and working part time?

Well, it was hard. Damn hard, but it was also wonderful.

Out of 125 students in my class, I was one of only two young ladies in the whole group who had a "sidekick," but **you have to go for your goals even when it's hard**. No—especially when it's hard.

Billy and I were finally living under the same roof for the first time, and each day it felt a little less like we were playing house. I even learned how to cook a few meals that didn't involve ravioli or ramen noodles, thanks to Rachel Ray's *30-Minute Meals*. While my friends went to Jillian's, a local bar, to destress from the week, Tyler and I watched Disney movies and Spiderman in our PJs. When I had a day off and my friends were doing…well, I don't know what exactly…Tyler and I would go with my friend Jennifer and her son on playdates to the zoo or the park.

Many students formed study groups, and I had a select few friends who wouldn't abandon me. We would study at my place while Tyler walked around in his diaper coloring with my highlighter on the backs of the pages inside my open binder while we crammed.

If you want something bad enough, you improvise and you work hard, and there will be people in your life that will trudge through it with you if you let them.

I believe this, and at that point in my life, I thought that was everything. I still think it is very important, but in time, I also learned that being in line with God's plan is perhaps even more important than the effort you exert or the actions that you take.

I believe that God will open doors for you—but in order for you to go through them, you have to be open to his will. You have to be able to see them, and you have to be willing to move your legs to walk through them.

And if you are headed in the right direction and you can't seem to make it the last mile, He will carry you the rest of the way. I believe in destiny, I believe in God's intervention on our behalf, but I also believe *God created us to do.*

Is there rain in the forecast?

If I were to pinpoint when the gray skies of my second storm started to roll in, I'd say it all started with our laughing blue-eyed baby running in the water of our sprinkler on a hot August day. I loved watching him clap his hands over the flying droplets and run back and forth through the streams of splashing cold.

He loved to run. Even when he was only a couple of months old, he would lie on the bed and kick his legs so fast it seemed impossible, like he was a superhero baby running midair, like if Flash were an actual person and had had offspring or reincarnated himself. My mom and I could barely control our laughter around him, primarily because he was so contagiously happy, but also because it was apparent that when he eventually made it vertical, I would never be able to catch him.

But at nearly two years old, even the quickest of babies are not without an accident or two. Tyler tripped on the sprinkler that day. As I scooped him up to kiss his fat little cheeks and the newly developing boo-boo on his little right foot, I took him in to dry him off and survey the damage. It was just a scrape, some bruising, and a little swelling. Nothing that would even warrant an ice pack or bandage and with a cold sippy cup of juice and a few minutes to settle down, there were no more tears.

Life was busy.

As I started my second year of pharmacy school, class was a full-time endeavor. I worked a weekend or two per month in a local pharmacy. Primarily, I spent the evenings after school pushing Tyler on the swing in the backyard or doing what moms do, get groceries, do laundry, cook dinner (or pick up the takeout), and when Tyler finally fell asleep for the night, then I would study. Of course, sometimes, I had to wake up super early in the morning and study or study during naptime. But in general, I didn't want to take away from my mommy time to do other things, so I juggled.

It was a couple of weeks later and a quiet afternoon. It was warm by the window, and I was basking in the opportunity to hold Tyler in the rocking recliner while he napped. His belly was pressed to mine and his head lay on my chest as he slept soundly.

This little guy was my motivation now.

Before he came along, I wanted to succeed for me. I wanted recognition. I wanted pride. Honestly, I felt I had to prove my worth. And also, I was greedy.

With Tyler in my life, I just wanted to give him the best life I possibly could. I wanted to work hard so I could provide everything he needed. I wanted to ensure Billy wouldn't have to take care of me, even though he was capable. I wanted to be a contributor to the family. I didn't want the vulnerability of feeling like I needed to rely on Billy or anybody else to survive.

I loved being a mom, but I felt I could be a great mom and have a great career, too!

Maybe I didn't plan on having a child in college but I was proving to myself that I could do anything with motivation and hard work. I began to feel at peace with my progress and full of love and gratitude to God for my new little family. But I still hadn't stopped for a moment to recognize my lack of relationship with God. I certainly didn't take time to seek God's guidance for direction for our lives. I wasn't leaning in on him.

These moments snuggling into Tyler's soft little body were now what made me proud and grateful…and just happy.

That's when I saw it.

As I rocked, stroking his back, sweeping his soft baby hair through my fingers, I noticed the slight swelling in that little right foot. It had been two weeks since the sprinkler incident and the bruising and scrape were gone. I'm not sure what drove me to do it, but I squeezed his foot, and that's when I felt it. It was a knot, a small knot buried inside his precious little foot. I called the pediatrician.

He was due for shots, and I love killing two birds with one stone. I needed the doctor to look at this.

I reasoned through everything I had been taught so far and thought maybe it could be a cyst caused by inflammation from the injury. While the doctor agreed that was a possible scenario, she added, "You only get one set of feet, and we are not taking chances. I am ordering an MRI."

I made my baby cry!

The MRI was slightly traumatic—for me. We did it at an outpatient facility. Tyler had to be asleep during the procedure, so the physician sedated him with chloral hydrate. The stuff tastes terrible. The second after he swallowed it, he started to cry.

Not just a regular cry but like he was terrified and then all of a sudden he was out. *I had made him cry*, essentially on purpose, so the doctors could do what they needed to with him. I felt horrible about this, like I was offering him up for a sacrifice to the "medical gods." I was worried; no, I was *scared*, and I just made my sweet baby cry.

It was the first time, but it would not be the last.

My mother-in-law was with us that day. She sat in the waiting area with

Billy. I sat at Tyler's side, holding his limp hand as he slept through the scan. It seemed like an eternity. Afterwards we were sent to another waiting area.

It was a little more private with a television that served as an ineffective means of distraction during the wait, and as Tyler woke up, we gave him a little bit to drink and held him as he came out of his grogginess. We sat without conversation, all three of us staring into space.

It was as if we weren't each worrying, but instead, **worry and fear held its own presence in the room**. It was strong enough to stand alone, not needing permission for the power it held over all of us but just taking it.

When the radiologist came in to talk to us, he was quick and to the point. Tyler had a tumor. He said it looked similar to some calcified benign tumor growths he'd seen, but he couldn't say for sure.

He could offer a referral to an orthopedic clinic and get us an appointment. That was it.

It wasn't a long drive home, 20 minutes, maybe. We didn't say much. We all cried nearly the whole way to our house. Not wailing weeping cries, just quiet sobs of despair, hot tears on our faces. We were uncertain about the future, but Tyler just cuddled me.

No questions, no complaints. He trusted we would take care of his every need. And that's what we did, the best we could, one day at a time.

"When the bough breaks the cradle will fall, and…"

Have you ever had a memory that plays back in your head like a movie, the colors as vivid as if they're in HD, the sounds are surrounding you?

That's how this next one is for me—when the bough broke. And even though I know how it all turns out, every time I think back, I feel my palms begin to sweat. My heart begins to race and my fists close tight as if I don't know what's coming next.

It was a sunny day. I'm sure I remember that clearly. It's hard for me to say for sure, though, whether or not it was raining through the sunshine. Or maybe my mind was confused by the stream of tears that clouded my vision.

It started harmlessly enough.

I was driving home from school. We got out early that day and it was a short trip, so I planned to stop by a nearby church with a reputable childcare learning program to see if they had any openings for Tyler. I had several friends who were singing its praises.

He would be two years old soon. Tyler had already had surgery to remove the tumor from his foot. We'd been told it was benign, and we would work on letting him heal.

I was listening to the radio when my phone rang.

It was Billy on the other end. I answered in a carefree way, my words spilling out about where I was going, how great it was to get out early, and asking what he wanted for dinner.

The voice that interrupted me hit me like a hammer. He sounded scared and angry.

THE BAD NEWS WAS LIKE A HEAD-ON COLLISION.

He told me to stop talking—he had bad news. "The doctor just called," he said, "and *Tyler has cancer.*" Plain and simple.

Then he started to cry (which I really had only seen happen a couple of times, like after the scans and at his grandmother's funeral), and said to hurry up and come home.

I could barely process anything past that moment. I was in disbelief. It was too horrible to hear.

I don't even remember hanging up. I just remember starting to cry as I pulled over to call my mom at work. I managed to compose myself as the phone rang.

My voice was cracking as I was trying to hold myself together for just one more minute when the lady answered the phone.

I asked for my mom, and she said, "I'll go get her, but you sound upset. Is everything okay?"

"My baby has cancer and I need my mom!" I felt frantic. I blurted out, "Would you please get my mom?!?"

Now in the niceties of the South, I never would have responded that way under other circumstances, risking dignity and all. It was the only glimpse an outsider would get of me "losing my sh*t."

Looking back now, I think how strong Billy had to be to take that phone call from the doctor's office. And then to be able to call me and relay the information. Selfishly, I'm still glad they didn't call me first.

I think about the people who sat across the desk from a doctor or nurse and heard the worst news of their life. While I know that's the most personal thing a healthcare provider can do, and they are there to offer kind words and empathy, I'm truly grateful to not have heard the news from strangers at that moment in my life. I know that no matter how strong I could ever possibly try to be, I would have fallen to pieces and felt my dignity disintegrate.

We hold ourselves to a much greater standard than we do others, of course.

It's human to be vulnerable, to be able to be damaged, and when we see this happen to someone else, we don't think less of them. Our hearts break for them.

We find the broken response to be the acceptable one, and we don't expect any other reaction. Yet we hold ourselves to this unrealistic standard of superhero strength.

We think that we are weak if we are not stoic.

And that's simply *not* true. I hope that one of the things I have taken away from this whole experience, and I think that I have, is to be fair to myself. I still hold myself to high expectations, but I hope to realize that I'm not invincible and that no one expects me to be. Also, allowing myself to learn to feel has not only been empowering, but also such a relief.

Even the *Bible* gives significant mention to human emotion. *"When we heard it, our hearts melted and no courage remained in any man any longer…"* (Joshua 2:11). *"Anxiety in a man's heart weighs it down, but a good word makes it glad"* (Proverbs 12:25).

There are so many verses displaying man's emotional flux. The *Bible* describes King David as a strong and powerful man but also deeply emotional. Even Jesus wept.

Never be ashamed to feel, or of how you feel, because you fear someone else will find you weak or judge your response or believe your feelings are irrational. Remember that all feelings are valid because they are real and they are yours.

It's amazing how a vivid memory can hold so much power.

It's been 15 years since that day, and as I think back, my stomach knots, my jaw clenches, and my eyes tear. It's over.

The danger of that day a million miles away and yet it's still there.

I lived through the story, and I know how it ends.

I completely understand how posttraumatic stress can have such a strong hold on those who have been victimized, on those who have seen awful things happen around them or to them.

While we can change the next chapter of our life, we are like a book that's being written every day. Just as we can't go back and change the days before, neither can we change the words on the pages that are already filled. There they are, never to be erased and available to view any time we choose, even those things that we try to block out.

All it takes is a certain smell, certain song or sound, a glimpse at a familiar face or of an item from that time, and we are transported back there instantly, whether we want to go or not.

The key is not letting it consume you and understanding that it's past.

Even if it was bad, evaluate what you learned from it, and how it bettered you. How can you help others get through what they are going through because of where you have been?

And so the spiral began.

Truly after that day, our life was never the same. In the days that followed, Tyler underwent a barrage of medical tests at the pediatric cancer hospital. I felt like a victim of a burglary, and at the same time like I was robbing my child. While I still had memories of happy moments in Tyler's childhood, my baby didn't get to be a baby anymore. I expected so much of him. I expected him to be still, to behave, to be polite, and not whiney or cranky over those very long, tiring, stressful, and sometimes scary days. And he was two.

The hospital was decorated in happiness, and the nurses were loving and friendly, which helped to distract our little guy from what was happening. From the moment the tests started, to placing the port in his chest, to witnessing the uncontrollable nausea from the chemo, we went through the motions.

Sometimes we could chat and return the smiles from hospital workers and other families in the waiting room, the cafeteria, and in the halls like everything was normal. Even when we felt sad, what good would it do us to make everyone around us sad? More importantly, to make Tyler sad?

Unacceptable.

We would be strong, as stable as concrete.

I feel bad about that now.

Making him hold still for every needle poke, holding his hands before each sedation. All the while, I felt a little bit like I was betraying him. I went through every motion and always trying to be strong, I asked Tyler to behave because I knew the nurses and doctors had hard jobs, and I didn't want to cause more stress in their day.

I think I believed that any other way showed vulnerabilities. I think I was still concerned about what impression we left.

I know if I were in their role, I would be understanding of a few tears, apprehension, and in general what were just outright cranky days, but I didn't allow myself those luxuries. Nor did I allow Tyler those luxuries, and for that I also feel bad.

I don't know that it could have been any other way. If I had let him bawl loudly when he felt like it, we would be disruptive to patient care. If I had let him be rude when he wanted to be cranky, what would that accomplish? What if he had wanted to fight and cry when he needed a new IV or sedation? Struggling against it couldn't have kept it from happening. But I still feel guilt somehow for not allowing him to just express his feelings, and I feel sad that even at two years old, he could not be carefree.

I remember him carrying fluid in his toddler-sized backpack so he could be more mobile while hooked up. I remember the days in the waiting area playing with the other kids. I remember studying to take my mind off things and get through school because that would be a way that I could take care of him and help Billy provide for our family. These were things I could control.

I couldn't control the cancer.

But I could ask questions. I could read about the cancer, and learn as much about it as possible. I could make sure we were still "good patients." I could make sure that I was a good student and a loving mom. But I couldn't control what was going to happen to Tyler.

Sometimes concrete cracks.

Just after the diagnosis of malignancy, I had to miss some classes for treatments and doctor appointments. It was very important to me to continue my coursework, for me to prove I could do it, to be productive, and as a distraction from the rest of my life for a short period of my day.

When I was in class, I could control my emotions. I was focused on what I needed to learn and what needed to be done. I still didn't know how to lean in on God or on others.

On one of my first days back, I was standing in the hall after class. My closest friends were beside me, genuine concern on their faces as they asked me for the latest news.

They knew we had started treatment. They cared about me. Before this all happened, they had studied with me. They had laughed with me. We had lunch together. A couple of these dear friends I had known from undergrad.

I felt their love and empathy. They were not trying to pry, but they needed me to know I wasn't alone.

It was more than I could take.

I tried to say, "When I found out Tyler had the tumor, I said we could handle the surgery. I told myself, as long as it's not cancer, this will be ok."

I began to feel my eyes well and I covered my face as I stammered. "But now that it's cancer, what do I say? How could it be worse?"

It was the first crack in the concrete. It was the trickle in the dam trying to weaken the whole structure. You never see that trickle when you're looking down from the rail. It was difficult at first, trying to stay positive, but up until this point, I always tried to look on the bright side of things.

Where is the silver lining, when things surely cannot get worse?

When my dad left, I thought, at least I have my friends, my sister, a home, my grandparents, etc. When Tyler was born so early, I thought, at least he wasn't sick, and I got extra time off for us to bond. When we found the tumor, at least it wasn't dangerous.

But once I was at the point where I thought it was the worst possible scenario, I didn't know what to do.

Billy was a rock, though. We are so fortunate he worked at such a great police department. His colleagues always showed us how much they cared. They donated their sick leave and made visits to see how we were doing. Billy was able to be with us every day we had to go for treatments and for every surgery.

He was quiet sometimes but not outwardly upset. He helped to keep Tyler occupied while we waited. I have known of many marriages that suffered, sometimes beyond repair, as they fought the battle of childhood cancer, but we grew closer. He was my best friend, and the serious circumstances we faced forced us to mature in many ways. We learned to put all pettiness aside and bonded together, allowing each other to lean in a way that we didn't lean on others.

When I think back to my emotional state then, I wonder if I was just too stressed and too scared to process everything. I wonder if maybe I was just going through the motions of life at that time. I wasn't exactly ignoring what we were going through but just taking it day by day, treating that day as a leg of the journey.

I couldn't see the end. I didn't know how many miles we had to go, but **if I just could make it 'til bedtime…**

The most terrifying thing was feeling there was no controlling what happened next, what happened tomorrow. It was like being sucked into a tornado.

I remember my breaking point.

My mom came to visit. They had told us the chemotherapy was not working and we would have to start to consider our options.

I felt this huge weight, the burden of decision, the responsibility of holding my life together, and the desire to save my child from all of this (which I couldn't do, of course).

I had been praying since Tyler was diagnosed that God would heal him. I envisioned going in for scans one day and being told the tumor had just gone. I didn't care if it were through a miracle or the right medication. I just wanted Tyler to be well and for this to be like a bad dream that we could shake off in the morning. I was holding onto the belief that the healing was the only fathomable solution to all of this.

My mom and I sat across from each other on my bed. My mom wanted to pray together. I don't remember what I said or wanted to say when the dam broke. I was sitting cross-legged with my face buried into the pillow.

I had never cried like that before and haven't since then. It was like being ripped apart or what I imagine a seizure might feel like. I couldn't breathe as the wails tore through me.

My eyes flooded with all the pain and anxiety and worry and despair I had been hiding for the last couple of months. When my face was tired from the fake smiles some days, now, my head ached from the furiousness of the flood of emotion that poured out of me.

I don't know how long it lasted. But when it subsided like a river finally leveling after the floodgate had been let down, I was exhausted and relieved. And it was in this moment, that I realized I had to have faith in whatever God's will was for Tyler. I had to be at peace with it, even if that meant he was not going to survive this. I was not in control.

> *"Life will break you. Nobody can protect you from that, and living alone won't either, for solitude will also break you with its yearning. You have to love. You have to feel. It is the reason you are here on earth. You are here to risk your heart. You are here to be swallowed up. And when it happens that you are broken, or betrayed, or left, or hurt, or death brushes near, let yourself sit by an apple tree and listen to the apples falling all around you in heaps, wasting their sweetness. Tell yourself you tasted as many as you could."*

> —Louise Erdrich

When we look back at our lives, do we see it as more than just a chronological collage of those day-to-day stretches that together yield a journey? Who are we really if not the culmination of our experiences? A series of these memories, some more impactful and lasting than others, paints the picture that is us.

When we leave this world, what will we leave behind? Will it be only the memory of us, engrained in the minds of those who were fortunate to know us while we were here? Or maybe our pictures in a photo album, or in a box on the shelf collecting dust? Or an online candid that will pop up in the memory feeds of our friends and family for a few years?

We have one chance to make the life we have deeper than that.

We have to live aware. We have to take the lemons we are given and make lemonade. I don't mean we simply strive to "get through" the tough times. I mean we process them, react to them, find purpose in them, and come out the other side better than before.

Think about it like a meat grinder. A little gross I know, but it's the best analogy I can think of.

There are all these big pieces of life that come at us and we have to take it in. We have to grind it up and make it something usable, something edible.

Seek God for understanding and for strength. Be confident you have purpose, and whatever you are going through will become a part of your testimony. It may be what inspires you to impact others.

Your other alternative is what? Just to deflect. But even if you just simply deflect, the events in your life still change who you are.

If you deflect, or then avoid everything that happens except the good, it's still happening. Even though you think you're not processing, not letting it happen to you, it's still affecting you.

In essence, you're just hiding and that is in itself a choice and a response.

For everything that happens, we have the option to have faith. We can trust in God and react in a way to turn the destination into a beautiful place, one in which we live victorious and can see the purpose in the pain. **It may not end the way we would plan if we were drawing the map, but God can transform even what's meant to harm His people into a blessing.** It's just hard to see that when you are in the middle of the long stretch.

You See Me

HITTING ROCK BOTTOM
FORCES US TO LOOK UP

Sometimes it takes losing everything we thought was important to us to find we have everything that we need.

Sometimes we have to hit rock bottom before we will force ourselves to look up.

"Have I not commanded you? Be strong and courageous. Do not be frightened and do not be dismayed, for the Lord your God is with you wherever you go" (Joshua 1:9).

I had to learn I can only control my actions. The rest I have to give to God. What other choice do I have?

And if he knows my heart, when I feel lost, my intent means as much as my words, especially when that is all that I have left to give.

What do you say in a moment of desperation, a minute of panic?

I know you have been there, that second when a deer or dog darts in front of your car and some word or phrase shoots out of your mouth too quickly for you to filter or even comprehend what you are saying.

For my dear friend since kindergarten, her word is "SUGAR!!!"

Others may resort to a word of the four-letter variety, and I don't mean "love."

The things we do or say based on instinct may reveal more about us than we realize.

Now believe me when I say that I have uttered my share of obscenities. I am most certainly not saying that if your impulsive response to panic is "OH SH*T!!" that you might be hiding a Godless heathen under your layers. But maybe thinking about what we say in these moments can give you a glimpse of the habits we are building into our subconscious. And it might allow you to meditate on the focus of your heart.

Maybe it would make a difference in our sense of stability and security if our first habit is to turn to God even in the small things, over trying to depend on ourselves or others.

Ever heard the song "Jesus Take the Wheel?" You get the idea.

What can I say?

Some people have been taught or raised to think that because God is this awesome, Almighty being, He is worthy of our best and our utmost respect. Some might extrapolate this to conclude that we can't communicate with

Him directly. Others think when we pray, it needs to be some well planned, drawn-out dictation in which the words must be perfect, reference *Bible* verses, and rival lectures heard in the seats of a philosophy class at Harvard.

I don't agree that all that is necessary.

I will say that one of the traits I pride myself in is my ability to be elegantly articulate when the moment calls. In other terms, I can dang well throw some words together and make it sound like a little somethin', feel me?

But, I feel like I am not alone, in that I truly can be at a loss for words *when my head is spinning with panic and my heart is desperate*, and I am feeling like Peter sinking in the waves, or like Jonah, when he really screwed up that time running away from God's will and ended up getting thrown out of that boat, and then God sent that whale to swallow him up to save his backsliding behind.

I need to know that God loves me and knows me so well, that my prayers can be simple, that *He knows the desire of my heart*, when I don't even know how to pray.

The *Bible* confirms that He does in Romans 8:26–27: *Likewise the Spirit also helpeth our infirmities: for we know not what we should pray for as we ought: but the Spirit itself maketh intercession for us with groanings which cannot be uttered. And he that searcheth the hearts knoweth what is the mind of the Spirit, because he maketh intercession for the saints according to the will of God.*

But feeling like I can still communicate with God helps me feel more secure, like I am doing all that I can, so I have a "go-to" prayer.

I wish I had known!

When you feel like you are drowning, you can let go of the circumstance dragging you down and cling to God as your lifeline. I wish this was something I knew back then, back when Tyler was sick, but it was something I had to learn in time.

I think about the day I needed it most—the day of Tyler's amputation.

Up to this point, I felt we had been broken already. I wanted all of it to go away but it seemed to just get worse, like a bad dream we couldn't wake up from.

On Christmas Eve, we had the scans that revealed the chemo wasn't working enough. The gift in that was that we wouldn't have to spend the holiday wondering and waiting for the test results. That part was always so hard. We would rather just know. But this time, *knowing* was equally as hard.

From that day on, we were on a train that wouldn't slow down. We were presented with a few options for his path to potential remission. Tyler's tumor had been analyzed by five pathology departments and we still did not have a firm definitive tumor type, so we were venturing into uncharted territory. None of them felt good to a pair of scared young parents.

One option was radiation with rods installed into his foot. It would be painful. We had no guarantees that the tumor would respond, and there was the possibility that the result would be a foot that wouldn't grow properly. Then, we might face amputation later. Could we risk leaving a fast-growing, chemo-resistant tumor inside his body?

The second option was amputation. We had never known another child amputee. This prospect seemed dismal. Getting the primary tumor and its surrounding tissue out of his body as quickly as possible sounded like a wonderful thing of course, but this option meant choosing for Tyler to be permanently disabled. He was still only two.

If he was lucky enough to make it through this, would he be able to play sports? Would kids make fun of him? Would he be able to grow up to be a functional adult? We honestly had no idea what to expect long term.

If we decided this for him, would he hate us for his handicap someday? What opportunities would he lose if we chose this for him?

The emotional weight of the pressure of this decision was almost physical in nature.

We knew that the option that made the most sense was to amputate Tyler's tiny right leg below the knee. We should be happy that we had that option. I kept telling myself that this was a good thing, like a saving grace, that we would get to save him maybe and just at the expense of his foot.

But this little boy, my little boy, so dearly loved to run.

How could this be happening?

My grandmother was long-time friends with a missionary who, at the time, was in his '80s. He had visited 99 countries spreading God's word. When Tyler first became sick, this missionary friend prayed and prophesied to my mom and grandma that Tyler would be well and would run. He wouldn't just run, our friend said, but he'd run fast, like a guinea. (I thought, "Isn't a guinea a bird? Surely he is confused!" But two years ago, I saw my first guinea, and he was right: they are crazy fast!)

As we heard the new devastating news, I thought about how I hoped and trusted God to heal Tyler. Now I felt like the clock was truly ticking, ticking toward the date and time of surgery, and this prophecy must be wrong, or maybe he meant he would run in heaven. To a mom forced to imagine a world without her baby, how scary that thought was. I thought about everything I had ever heard about God's healing and miracles.

I was glad miracles happened to other people, but why, oh why, couldn't they happen for us?

Just this one time, if He could answer my prayer, I would never pray for anything again or I would pray for everyone else and do and be anything He wanted me to be.

I felt desperate.

Doomsday.

February 2, 2004 was the hardest day of my entire life. Billy and I brought Tyler to the hospital early that morning. I felt sick. My desperation had reached a new level, not the panicked level, but passed that to the inevitable doom-type feeling.

I kept hoping, as each minute crept us closer to "op time," that there would be some kind of divine intervention or delay.

Maybe they would go to check him in and realize they didn't have him scheduled! Nope, all went smoothly.

Maybe the surgeon or the anesthesiologist would be sick today! Nope, they were there, smiling and reassuring.

Or maybe they would do a final exam and find that the tumor was miraculously gone. But that didn't happen either.

Billy and I tried to act as normal as possible. We didn't want Tyler to be upset or scared. We did, however, want to be sure he didn't wake up feeling betrayed. He was only two and a half but we felt we only had each other and our trust.

Before they took him into the operating room, we held his little hands. We told him that we loved him. "Remember how your foot is making you sick? Well, the doctor is going to have to do surgery to take it away so you can be better." He started to cry a little and we told him we would get him another foot, like a robot foot, that would be strong, and maybe he would never be sick again.

Then we hugged him as tightly as we could and asked him if he wanted to race down the hall one more time, and that's what we did. He ran as fast as his little legs could carry him down the hall and back. I laughed but with sad tears in my eyes. I gave him another hug and big kiss, and then Billy went with him into the surgery suite while they put him to sleep.

When Billy came back to the waiting room, I was already bawling, and he joined me. We hugged each other, and we cried.

We cried for what we felt Tyler was losing: A normal, happy life. **We cried because we couldn't understand why this was happening**. We cried because it felt like such a profound tragedy. We cried because we felt like we had been taken out of our safe normal lives months ago and now were truly realizing that we had been totally and utterly abandoned by God. I had no words. I had no prayers. **I felt empty in that moment**, and it seemed the prophecy was wrong. My son surely would not run.

MY PRAYER

Now when I feel the grips of desperation try to creep into my mind and fog my focus, quite simply my prayer, my desperate cry to God, is composed of three little words. And no, it's not "I love you." Although that is true and maybe would be perfectly appropriate—I hope God extrapolates that from my prayer—but my prayer is this:

"YOU. SEE. ME."

You may wonder how this could be enough or what it means. You may wonder how God will know what on Earth I am asking for. So, I will tell you what it means to me. How each word is crucial to me. Why I think for me it works, aside from just being easy to repeat when I don't know what else to say.

YOU.

I need to first acknowledge that God is my provider, my Father, the only one who can help me, fix me, fix things. I proclaim that I rely on Him wholly and desperately. You. I am recognizing Him as Almighty. I am surrendering to Him. I trust Him to be loving and compassionate. I proclaim He is the center of my focus, and that my eyes, my heart, my mind must solely look to and lean into Him to lift me out of the quicksand I can't seem to pull out of.

The *Bible* says in Revelation 1:8, "'I am the Alpha and the Omega,' says the Lord God, 'who is and who was and who is to come, the Almighty.'" *You*, my Lord, are my creator and my salvation.

SEE.

I don't mean this in an open-your-eyes-and-look-at-me kind of way. Maybe more in the way that a toddler means when they say, "Look at me, look at me, look at me." They need not just your line of vision but also they need to hold your complete and full attention. They expect you to process what they are showing you, they want you to acknowledge them, and most of the time they also require an action from you.

Sometimes it is just praise and a hug. Other times, they want for you to fulfill a need, like give them a drink or a snack, or for you to engage with them in their favorite activity. Or also maybe they want affection and cuddle time during an episode of Mickey Mouse Clubhouse. But they demand it.

I mean see in this way, and also *maybe even more.*

See me in a way that I cannot see myself. See me as Psalms 139 describes: "You have searched me, Lord, and you know me…"

See into my heart. See into my future and know what's best for me and show me a glimpse of your presence and sovereign plan. I am requiring a response of action and of comfort and wisdom that I can't seem to provide for myself or find in any other place. See me by making me a priority and coming to my rescue right now!

See me like how a rescue chopper sees a flare in the ocean coming from my lifeboat. My lifeboat with a small leak surrounded by circling starved sharks as it gets dark.

Yes, my desperation has felt just like that.

ME:

God, you see me. *You created me.*

I am here, waving my white flag of surrender. I am your child. You love me. You know me, my inner thoughts and feelings that I share with no one, my destiny. *I need you*, in an urgent, I-literally-don't-know-what-to-do kind of way.

ME. With my strengths, weaknesses, experiences, and inadequacies, only you know what I can and cannot do, what I can and cannot withstand. And although the *Bible* says I can do all things through Christ who strengthens me, I do not feel strong, and I'm getting pretty near the end of my string with this one. So, I know YOU SEE ME!

So, maybe if you have had an instance of feeling too discouraged and overwhelmed to pray, or just want to prepare yourself for when that comes, try coming up with a small meaningful prayer.

Get with God and say, "Listen God, I love you and I know you hear me, so when I am losing myself, I am going to pray, just like this, and I need you to know what that means."

The truth is that He already knows how you feel, but I know communicating it makes me feel like I am doing something. I believe God wants us to reach out to Him!

The *Bible* has loads to say on this.

"And if we know that he hears us—whatever we ask according to His will—we know that we have what we asked of Him" (1 John 5:15).

"Look to the Lord and His strength, seek His face always" (1 Chronicles 6:21).

"Then you will call on me and come and pray to me, and I will listen to you" (Jeremiah 29:12).

"I will call on you, my God, for you will answer me, turn your ear to me and hear my prayer" (Psalm 17:6).

MY PRAISE.

This has also become my praise when I am too overwhelmed with joy and adoration from God's provision. Just as "aloha" is both hello and goodbye in Hawaii, "You see me!" really carries the meaning that I needed you, you saw me, you heard me, you provided; and I am so thankful and overwhelmed because you really do see me in every way that I meant it and prayed for it. The provision may not have been in the way that I envisioned or expected but you prove yourself to be my loving Father and my provider, just as your Hebrew names Abba and Jireh describe.

It is my way to give him a huge hug or high-five the only way I can. It's like saying, "You see me!" i.e., "Way to frickin' go, God, coming through for me *again*! Why on Earth do I ever worry? Seriously!"

Later that desperate day, the day of amputation, we went down and hugged and updated those who refused to stay away or whom we didn't have the heart to tell not to come. Our pastor, who was also the chaplain at the police department, my mom and stepdad, Billy's uncle and aunt, my in-laws, and others, I think, were among the crowd there in the lobby waiting area.

I feel grateful for the love of everyone that came, but when I think back everything was hazed with pain and sadness and I don't even remember all the faces or embraces or prayers that greeted me that day.

When we went back up to the surgery waiting room to wait for word that everything was going well, we were out of tears. We met another family who was just starting their journey. Madelyn got her port put in that day to start chemo. She was Tyler's age, and she and her family would become near and dear to our hearts. Despite being wrung out from the emotion of the day, we found a little comfort in bonding with them.

When surgery was over, we were taken to the ICU, and our friends Todd and Dawn were allowed to join us soon after. They were the only visitors we allowed into our most vulnerable place. Along a hall lined with rooms identical to ours with other families in them dealing with circumstances that were just as frightening and dismal as ours, Todd and Dawn were the glimpse of hope we needed. We talked and laughed and reminisced and prayed while Tyler slept. They had lost their son in this same ICU hall only a few years before. Some of the nurses that took care of us even remembered them and gave them hugs. But they were there for us and they were strong.

Seeing their strength and continued faith after the loss of Shae, their son, I realized that whatever was to come, God did see me. I didn't know what was coming next, but I knew that I wouldn't always understand His plan. **I had to be okay with that,** and know that His plan was divine, and may be different than my own.

CELEBRATION AND REMEMBRANCE

It was the worst, most desperate day of my life but we celebrate it every year as the end of Tyler's cancer.

Just a few short years later, on a February 2, the anniversary of the start of her treatment and the end of Tyler's, Madelyn passed. We celebrate Tyler's second chance, yes, but we also remember Madelyn every year and we celebrate that we were lucky enough to be her friends in her short time on Earth. We celebrate that she is pain free and well in heaven, even while we are sad that all of us here, especially her precious family, have to miss her.

So, whatever your prayer is, know God already has everything all laid out.

Feeling overwhelmed and desperate and scared is human, but the *Bible* says God wants us to rely and lean on Him and not our own understanding.

That feeling of desperation will not change the situation but your reactions and your reliance on God can change some things. It can change your heart, it can help strengthen you, it can help strengthen others.

Communication with God is never futile, and **I do still believe miracles happen, even if my miracle didn't look the way I thought I wanted it to.**

And while it is not unique to worry, you are made uniquely and beautifully. God made you that way, so He doesn't expect for us to be the same. We all communicate with each other in our own way. Who says we have to pray the same way? Whether you talk to God like a parent or your pastor or your best friend, the *Bible* says we are made in His image and He wants us to lean on Him and talk to Him.

Your relationship with God is between you and Him (or perhaps the Holy Trinity), but nobody else, so put aside your preconceived ideas about what that's supposed to look like. **You do you**, just like He created you to be, and you might find it a lot easier and more rewarding than you would have guessed.

Regardless of your background and upbringing, regardless of your level of knowledge about the *Bible* and religious history, God accepts you into his fold. Accepting Him into your heart, salvation, is what matters. It's the first step. And the rest—learning about God's word, recognizing God's will, fellowship with others—that is just part of the guidebook for your journey. Expect to sometimes feel lost along the way but know that if you have given your heart to God, you never are out of his watchful protection.

You will look back and see His grace was there, even when you didn't feel it.

You Are Not Alone

WHETHER YOU LIKE IT OR NOT, AND WHY THAT MATTERS

Empathy is somehow more meaningful than sympathy.

As humans, we often alienate ourselves when we're going through something hard. We tend to think nobody can possibly understand.

Nobody has been where we have been.

No one has gone through what we have gone through.

We put ourselves on another planet mentally, simply called "our own world." You've heard the term.

While our circumstances might seem grim and, by all means, unique compared to those we know, I propose that while each one of us is special, our trials and tribulations are not as unique as we imagine.

Nobody knows what I am going through.

When we received Tyler's diagnosis, in *my* little world, I had never known another child with cancer. I'd never met an amputee, aside from when Billy's grandmother lost her leg shortly before she lost her life, and to be quite honest, we were terrified and felt like there was not a single soul who would understand.

Close family were devastated as well, and it didn't help to talk to friends most of the time because they just looked at us with those sad eyes. They loved us and felt sorry for us, but overall, they didn't know what to say to make things better. Of course, they didn't. What could they say that would fix things? It was like we were a racehorse with a broken leg.

We were once a happy family and were now in danger of being put out to pasture or shot.

Is it something I did?

Making the decision for amputation is likely the hardest decision we have made in our lives. We understood the permanent impact, but we also knew we could not predict the outcome of other treatment options. We were terrified of the risks of Tyler living with this ominous disease inside his body, and I wondered if there was perhaps just still one seed of doubt in my heart that was the reason God did not heal Tyler. How would I find, and extricate, that seed of doubt? How do I accept the blessing of God's healing for Tyler? **I still desperately wanted a miracle and what if my actions were somehow inhibiting it?** Heavy stuff for a 22-year-old.

There were others in my family who also questioned my decisions and my faith, which compounded my insecurities. Some suggested that scheduling an amputation for Tyler was robbing God's opportunity to heal him. I felt like I was looking at three doors, and I could only choose one. Two meant death and one led to life, but they all looked exactly the same. I felt my analytical skills were failing me. I felt the faith I had managed to muster was failing me. I was blind while I had to find my way through an unfamiliar place, searching for a way out.

I was weary in my still-young faith and began to continue to question God. How could He let him go through this? How could He let this happen to us? Was I truly being punished? Was my faith just not strong enough? If miracles happen, why wouldn't He do it for Tyler?

These are all very difficult feelings independently, and Billy and I struggled to stay optimistic in the turmoil. I had to set aside the judgments and those feelings. I had to realize that no matter what was to come, I had to believe it was God's will.

It was the scariest but most freeing revelation.

"If I can do it, you can do it."

We were yearning for someone to say, "I have been there. I know what you are feeling, and you will make it through this because I did. I am proof."

I know now that my individual struggles are not in themselves unique.

Some startling facts:

> According to the American Childhood Cancer Organization, in 2014, an estimated 15,780 children and adolescents ages 0 to 19 years will be diagnosed with cancer in the United States alone. That means roughly one out of every 285 U.S. kids get cancer. Globally, the number is 300,000 children diagnosed annually. If you do the math, that's a new family affected every 3 minutes. (ACCO.org)

It is the second leading cause of death in children one to 16 years of age in the U.S., behind accidents. (ACCO.org)

The Amputee Coalition of America reports there are nearly two million people living with limb loss in the United States. (amputee-coalition.org)

Approximately 185,000 amputations occur in the United States each year. (amputee-coalition.org)

At the time, these people affected by cancer and loss were strangers to me. It was as if they didn't matter or exist. I was on that other planet and my rocket was out of commission.

I didn't want to be inspiring.

According to Google, the definition of inspiring is "to fill someone with the urge or ability to do or feel something."

I didn't want to be "inspiring." I felt that being inspiring simply meant that bad sh*t was happening to me and good for me that I didn't just roll over and die.

I didn't want to be pitied.

Just make it go away...

Each day at the hospital, we watched Tyler play in the waiting area. Billy and I took turns playing with him while the other sulked. We wanted him to feel happy and normal, even though things weren't normal. Even when Tyler wasn't feeling well, he always wanted to socialize. Even when we were feeling moody (we would still smile politely at everyone around, of course), he wanted to socialize.

Yet we still felt alone. We made a couple of dear friends through this daily hospital experience. Mostly, though, I didn't feel I needed to connect with other families.

I needed to be there and do what we needed to do for Tyler, to try and fix this thing, but I mainly wanted it to all go away like it never happened. **And it was sad**. Like we were all in line to be beheaded. So, I preferred not to talk about it.

I didn't know the value of empathy yet. I had fear. I fought feelings of hopelessness and denial. I was just becoming an adult. I was still a new mom. Struggles of this magnitude were not only unexpected but almost incomprehensible, yet here we were.

And what's more, I was ashamed of these feelings that made me appear weak and vulnerable, pitiful even, so I just avoided conversations. Hiding them with silence seemed easier than covering them up with superficial, pretentious chat. I was far too exhausted to proactively appear positive all the time.

I kept it factual and optimistic when I had to talk about it, like a news anchor talking about some tragedy, or a car salesman trying to sell a big broke-down lemon. I didn't really want to make friends there because I didn't feel better or consoled by seeing them suffer like me at the time.

I needed a success story to inspire me.

It took some time, but after a bit into Tyler's treatment, we learned to lean a little on one of Billy's colleagues and his wife. Todd and Dawn were the ones we allowed to come to the ICU after Tyler's amputation. Their experience with childhood illness had happened roughly three years prior. Billy had been at the funeral. Their angel flew away in the very hospital we were receiving treatment.

I was in awe of them when they sat with us in the ICU at Tyler's bedside after the amputation.

There is comfort in feeling a similarity or kinship to others who had come out of the storm and made it.

I couldn't quite fathom how you could continue to live after your child was gone but they had. As difficult as it was to send Tyler to the surgery that would change his life forever, it had seemed to be the only alternative to "the worst that could happen." Here were these two, kind, strong people who had been through the worst, and yet they were sitting in a room on the same hall of the ICU where they lived with their son during his last breath, and they were there solely to comfort us.

And they weren't just there for us. They were a rock to many families dealing with cancer and other sicknesses through the charity they served. Back then I couldn't understand how they could see these other sick babies and not crumble at the memory. How could you ever be happy again? How could *I* ever be happy again? This was worse than my worst nightmare.

They were so strong.

Now I realize the value and the satisfaction in being able to show someone that they are not alone. Not alone to cope. Not the only one to ever suffer. **There is a mutual healing in helping.** Maybe, just maybe, if they could be strong, I could be strong even if this didn't go our way.

I am strong.

I don't share this story to get praise for my strength, even though I am strong. I don't share this story to gain pity for Tyler's loss, even though he suffered and things aren't always easy. I don't share this story because I want to live in the past, reliving that difficult time.

I tell it because I made it through, my family made it through, and we are stronger.

I tell it because whether your scars are too blatant for some to ignore or completely invisible to everyone but you, what doesn't kill you *can* make you stronger. I tell it to hopefully help you see that God gives you strength when you feel you cannot go on, and that if we act in His will, we will trust His plan for our life. He doesn't promise we will be free from adversity but we can find peace in knowing there is perhaps purpose in our pain and that God has not forsaken us.

The *Bible* gives us passages to encourage our strength in times of struggle and remind us that God has not abandoned us in our times of crisis:

"I can do all things through Christ which strengtheneth me" (Philippians 4:13).

"But the God of all grace, who hath called us unto His eternal glory by Christ Jesus, after that ye have suffered a while, make you perfect, stablish, strengthen, settle you" (1 Peter 5:10).

"For I know the thoughts that I think toward you, saith the Lord, thoughts of peace, and not of evil, to give you an expected end. Then shall ye call upon me, and ye shall go and pray unto me, and I will hearken unto you. And ye shall seek me, and find me, when ye shall search for me with all your heart" (Jeremiah 29:11–13).

If you look around, you will see that nearly everyone you know has at some point struggled through their own version of hell. If they haven't, then it's probably not their turn just yet.

And now…

Now, I feel differently about inspiration. So often, the word is used flippantly for anyone who accomplishes anything or publicizes being in a difficult situation, but truly being inspirational in its very basic definition has become my life's goal.

To me, being inspiring means that I can help someone feel the ability to prevail.

You can let your situation break you or you can use it to strengthen you. If you choose to use it for strength, then you can use what you've learned to help strengthen others so that you feel like you went through hell for a reason.

Being inspiring is about reminding people that even when they don't feel strong, they are; that even when it looks bad, there are others worse off; that they may be unique in their abilities, but they are not unique in their struggle. It is about showing others that it is within their control to look to God and not let their struggles tear down who they are but to allow these trials to mold them into something stronger, something brighter, like molten steel into a sword.

That is what inspiration is about. It's not easy, but it is worth it.

Locked in but not alone...

I thought I wanted to be out on our own planet when things were hard. I couldn't see it then but truly it was our community and connectedness that really helped me through. Not being alone, even when I thought we were, gave me comfort and support. My focus just wasn't there enough to recognize that.

Support came in lots of shapes from unexpected places now that I look back. Today, I bask in connection and community.

On the not-so-bad days, I looked forward to seeing other families in the waiting rooms and in the cafeteria. I hoped to hear good news about their situation. I loved them and prayed for them. I wanted to see their familiar faces and smiles.

Brother Steve, the chaplain at the police department, also pastored a church and the people of their congregation became a second family to us. Our relocation to Memphis meant we were almost two hours from our actual families and our home church, and we allowed these strangers in an inch or two at a time.

We weren't in an emotional or mental state to want to meet new people or to desire new relationships. Yet, they were generous and persistent with their love and prayers and acts of kindness, and while we were too tired to fight anything, we didn't fight that either. We inevitably let them in. I am grateful that we did.

Some of my friends from school brought me notes to help me study. One of my friends brought her son to play with Tyler when he was feeling well. Many checked in on me.

My mother-in-law came to stay with Tyler on days when Billy had to work and I needed to be in class. My mom came when both Billy and I had to work on weekends.

When Tyler was well enough to go to daycare, the teachers there loved us like family and we still stay in touch even though we have since relocated, and we keep up with each other on social media. I felt secure when he was there despite his newly found challenges.

He was one of the youngest amputee patients at St. Jude at the time and so we didn't get the opportunity to connect with another family in our same circumstances. It became very important for me early on that he had connection and bonding to see he was not alone in his differences.

I found an email list for parents of amputees called ICAN. It was my first glimpse of promise in the networking I desired. It was in those emails that I learned there were athletics for those with physical challenges, places for Tyler to make friends, camps and resources. We attended the first event with no idea what to expect and it changed our lives. Tyler would know that he was not alone in his struggles, not unique. **He would be surrounded by support.**

I would meet others that walked the path before me. I bonded with some of the other moms instantly. They have been the ones I call over and over when I am discouraged about a setback Tyler faces or to get advice on how they handled certain situations. They became "my people." And I've been able to give that to others over time.

No, you are not alone.

While you may feel stronger or safer behind the walls you have built around you, when you feel like peeking over them, you will see all the people surrounding you and lifting you up with love and prayer the entire time. They will be grateful when you decide to lean on them a little.

My friend, author Donita Brown, shares in her book the life lessons learned from her father. She writes that you should "always take the casserole." Allowing others to bless you is a blessing to them.

One of my favorite quotes on Pinterest that sums it up well is this: "*What God is bringing you through at this very moment is going to be the testimony that will bring somebody else through. **No mess, no message**.*" I don't know who the author is but this sentiment rings true for me.

Selfish

SOMETIMES IT'S JUST NOT ABOUT US

So, we are not alone, not in our struggle, and not without support. When we look around and see who is there for us, we realize how many others are facing these similar situations. We are not even alone in feeling alone.

This is where I challenge you to change your perspective. I want you to think about this in the midst of your difficult situation.

"This is not what I planned, and this is not what I wanted. But maybe this is not about me."

What if we made it our mission in every endeavor to draw the most out of the day? If we are not here tomorrow, maybe we can try to make it so that at least every person or thing we touched is better off than they were yesterday.

What I am about to say comes with the risk of offending all of my readers. Ready?

We are a selfish, self-centered, self-serving people as a whole, especially in this country.

There are exceptions, of course, but our norm is generations of people who are concerned primarily with:

What do I want to do?

What do I want to wear?

Who do I want to be?

What will I watch?

Where will I go?

How much money can I make?

Who do I want to be with?

How long will I have to wait?

And on and on. For most of us, **our world revolves around us**, even when **our impact** on the actual world may indeed be **minimal**.

This is our natural state since the fall of man, and if we are aware of this as our vice, it can become a constant battle we must be diligent to win.

Selfish...

When I was in fourth grade, my dad left, in a profoundly unforgettable, missing persons kind of way. He left nothing but a letter and my ability to trust has never been the same.

I don't tell this to make him look bad or feel bad. I want to share how every story has many characters. We each play a part but we each have some effect on others, some small, others large. **I only truly know my part.**

I remember when he came home finally. I have no idea if it was one day or many days or weeks. To me as a kid, it felt like forever. Really, he only came back for a few hours and then he didn't stay, but I sat in the living room at the door staring outside the entire time he was there.

I wanted him to know what it was like to know I was there but that I didn't want him to be there because he didn't want to be with me.

When he finally came to hug me goodbye, I stormed out stomping and crying that he didn't love me. *"Just go away and never come back!"*

I didn't mean that, and I was being very dramatic, but our story is always focused on us. **How we feel blurs out the rest of the periphery.** I didn't care to understand how my mom, my dad, or my baby sister felt. I didn't want to process the greater meaning of what having a broken family was to mean for us. At that moment, **it was all about my hurt.**

What changed?

As an adult, I didn't harbor hateful feelings for my dad but I did grow to be apathetic. I didn't want to try harder or care more in any relationship than the other person. I felt it wouldn't be fair. To me, my dad didn't try or care.

It has taken years and I finally feel like we are meeting in the middle. We don't talk every day but we talk. With time, I have grown to care again.

As a mom, a healthcare provider, a Christian, and through my journey of self-discovery in writing this book, if I am acknowledging that every moment has the ability to impact the rest of our life, this is true for even my own father.

Just because he is a parent, my parent, doesn't make him superhuman. He had a rough go as a kid—really, really rough, and even though he was eventually adopted by two of the most precious people I have ever met and was proud to call my grandparents, there were already wounds that might not ever heal and could potentially affect all other relationships he would ever have.

Can we start over?

In many ways, I see myself like a mirror of him. I have the ability to write people off, I can say the most cutting things when I am angry, and I would rather ignore you completely than work out a problem if I let my inner instincts rule. I also am driven and a hard worker and smart.

But then I realized one day, maybe I don't even know him really. Not as an adult and maybe my memory is a bit distorted. And honestly, he didn't know me either, and if we were in this place, a different place, a new day, why not start over?

As you're reading, you may be able to guess that I don't think our pain or fear gives us a "get out of jail free" card. But recognizing that his actions that resulted in my pain may have been a product of his own pain helps me relate to him and understand that his choices may have been made without giving me much consideration. I played a character that was affected, yes, but I wasn't the main character for him at the time in his story.

I don't know that he has ever apologized for what happened or if I just always failed to listen for one, but I feel resolved and at peace with our progress.

I recognize that I have been affected long term by the events. I know that my pursuit of independence, and fear of relying on others and on God during those vulnerable college years, was in part a product of my broken trust. When I was a new mom and Tyler had cancer, and I failed to rely on others, this, too, was a product of my broken trust.

74

Being brought up in a profoundly Christian environment, only to see sin dissolve the seams of what I thought was a happy household, resulted in my confusion over how our destiny is determined. I questioned whether God gets bothered with the details or if he is only concerned with salvation. And if everything is predetermined by God's plan, what is the purpose of free will or faith, and do they even exist?

But the beauty of life is reflected in our body's ability to heal. As long as we live to see another day, we can continue to emotionally, mentally, and spiritually evolve. Praying, seeking God's guidance through reading His word or through ministry, can help us piece together the things we can't seem to make sense of, especially in times of hurt.

I tell my dad I love him before I hang up now. His name is now saved in my phone with a parenthetical after it: (Dad). **And I don't have to be okay with feeling abandoned or forgotten** but I feel that my reaction to be receptive to his efforts of reconnection and moving forward from his mistakes are only fair if I expect to **move forward** from my own mistakes because he is human, too. And this has brought the healing I really wanted for the longest time, the healing that ignoring it never gave me.

We are selfish...

This is not an easy thing to absorb, especially when "the bad thing" is happening to you. When I was younger, during the most difficult situations I had to struggle through, I can attest that this was not my attitude. As stated, when my parents got a divorce, it was tragic to me. When I got pregnant, I thought about how this wasn't what I had planned and how it would affect *my* future. When Tyler was sick, I wondered why and how could this happen to us. It is the most natural response.

Survival mode, our most primitive state, is even geared toward taking care of number one.

Who cares how you feel?

I also didn't think or care so much, to be honest, about how things were affecting those around me.

I always tried to be strong for Billy when Tyler was sick, but I didn't want to deal with anyone else's feelings beyond that. **I could barely deal with my own.** Our parents, of course, were devastated as well, but I didn't want them to be around very much.

I didn't want to talk about it. I didn't want to think about it (unavoidable, by the way).

Most importantly, I didn't want to hear anyone else cry, or ask why, or show any kind of emotion over what was happening.

I wanted to feel, "This is happening to us, not to you, and I can't take care of you, too!"

We didn't really talk to friends about it. We didn't call people up and let them know. We became locked in our bubble. Two of my best friends found out thirdhand! Now I can't imagine how dumbfounded they must have been or how I would have felt in their shoes.

When Tyler began his first chemo treatments, my mom and my stepdad came to the hospital. My mom kept wanting to cry and pray and hug me. I wanted no part of that.

My stepdad told her privately, "Why did we come? She doesn't want us here."

I couldn't bear any more weight than my own. My mom didn't understand, and honestly, we never spoke about it until she read the first few draft chapters of this book. (Writing this and sharing it has been therapeutic on many levels.)

Let me tell you…

I can't say that I am remorseful over the way it happened. I dealt with it the best that I could. But I will say that now that I can look back and understand my reaction, I have been able to learn from what I've lived through, what I perceive now as being a suboptimal response. I use what I have learned from it to help strengthen me in my life and difficulties I face now.

I have learned two things I want you to take away from this chapter.

The first: If you are on the perimeter of a tragedy and it is affecting you, but you are being pushed away, understand **it has nothing to do with you**. My mom's feelings, and I am sure likewise those of many of our family and friends, were hurt. It was not my intention for them to feel hurt or left out, but I wasn't able to hold everything together and try to fix them, too.

So, if you are looking in, know it's not about you. The best thing you can do is be on standby in case you are needed. Sometimes mending together can only happen when both parties are ready and willing for that to happen. **Sometimes the best support is just the support that is offered gently and consistently but not forced.**

Check on them and make sure they are reminded your love and assistance is there when they do feel the urge to take it. If they don't answer, don't take it personally. Be specific in your offers of assistance. If you say "call me if you need me" they probably won't. Volunteer to babysit for an afternoon, get them a gift certificate for a massage or their favorite café, write thank-you cards for them to others who have helped them, clean their house or do their laundry, pick up their grocery order.

It really doesn't matter what you offer as long as it will help them. The day-to-day of the chaos of crisis is often overwhelming. Understand they may be a bit hesitant and may likely say no the first time you ask, but you can always offer again on another day. Remember if they don't say thank you, it doesn't mean they aren't incredibly grateful.

The second thing I learned is that my difficulty and how I deal with it may have a larger meaning or purpose. In short, it might not be about me. I realized this when Tyler was about five years old.

Our prosthetist arranged for Tyler to come in for his appointment at the same time as another new patient came for his fitting. The child was near his age and a newer amputee due to trauma. This boy had been through a difficult time and was a little reserved. Tyler didn't even notice this child was shy. He just started talking and laughing with him as if they had always been friends.

Within an hour they were hopping down the hall in their Underoos having a race!

That first time I saw him pull another child out of his shell, I realized something very special was happening. I realized our struggle was not in vain. I had this warm comforting feeling that Tyler had a purpose for his life that was bigger than him, bigger than me, bigger than his cancer, and bigger than his disability.

"Trust in the LORD with all your heart and lean not on your own understanding" (Proverbs 3:5).

Maybe it's not about me...

After that, my coping mechanism for every difficult situation involves reminding myself that perhaps my struggle is bigger than me.

Maybe it is meant for me to learn something that I will be able to share with someone else in their struggle.

Maybe it means that someone needs to be inspired by my strength to get through.

Maybe it means that I can make a change through persistence and perseverance that might ensure I prevent someone else the same mistreatment I experienced. Perhaps that someone might not have been able to push through it like me.

Maybe I might not see the significance for years or ever but **believing and grasping the hope that the reason is there, helps me through.**

Good Grief

ALL ABOUT GRIEF

My Marine friends have a saying, "Pain is weakness leaving the body."

If there is something to that, then the pain that grief brings has its purpose.

"Good grief."

Seems like an oxymoron, right? When is grief good? It definitely doesn't feel good. It usually comes from something bad.

What is grief anyway?

The definition of grief in the dictionary is "keen mental suffering or distress over affliction or loss; sharp sorrow; painful regret."

If we don't care about something and we lose it, we typically aren't sad. For us to grieve the loss, even if the thing we lose was something that overall wasn't good for us, the thing we lost had to have held some type of value to us for us to grieve for it.

We've already covered that we are not alone in our struggles and that loss is universal. Every one of us will experience it at some point during our lives. Some of us will have much bigger losses than others, but we will all have at least one impactful loss during our lives. Some losses are brought on by death, others are from the end of a relationship or job, or other phase of life.

Is all grief the same?

I've taken my fair share of leadership classes and personality tests, and I am nothing if not analytical. So, I find value in recognizing our situation, calling it what it is, so that we can somehow start to tackle the task of coping.

Different types of grief may need different strategies for moving through them and even though we may not understand why something *is*, it is essential to understand what exactly is happening, right?

So, let's give the following types of grief their 15 minutes of fame:

- Grief because we've lost something good in our life
- Grief because we've lost something that was bad for us
- Lament or regret
- Empathic grief

When good is lost:

The most obvious and the first we'll discuss: losing something good or someone you love.

This can happen through an unfortunate circumstance—a death, a divorce, a move, and so on. We grieve the absence and the feeling we have from knowing we'll never have it again. There is a longing. We feel sorry for ourselves.

Many times, the event is a traumatic occurrence, regardless of whether it was foreseen or took us completely by surprise. The losses we know are coming allow for us to prepare for them mentally and emotionally, but it is still sad and we still grieve.

My friend Angela, who was with me the night I met Billy at the gas station, lost her son to cancer in 2018.

I will never forget getting her call when she found out about the severity of their situation. I sat in my closet floor and cried as we talked on the phone about all the necessary next steps with the diagnosis of stage IV glioblastoma. I wanted to be strong and someone she could lean on, but I also just wanted to erase this from happening to her.

I knew the fear and despair that was shaking her and that the odds were not great. And even though I knew that somehow this was her path despite the fact we didn't understand it, I got to say for her, selfishly, "Dammit, this is *NOT FAIR!* And I don't want this to happen to Wesley."

TYLER AND WESLEY

When Tyler and Wesley were young, they were at St. Jude together. At the time, Wesley's tumors were benign and Tyler's was not. Over time, Wesley was treated to control the tumor growth in his brain and the side effects and seizures they caused but at least he didn't have cancer.

It was nearly 14 years later when new symptoms of hearing loss and vertigo signaled something might be wrong. Scans then revealed stage 4 brain cancer. Wesley's family and friends were blessed to have a whole year with him after the ominous diagnosis and after sharing many special moments knowing that their time together on Earth would be cut short, he passed peacefully surrounded by people who loved and adored and admired him.

Many have recognized the grace my sweet friend displays in public. Smiling and laughing when things are funny, going to watch her other boys play baseball, and going back to work. She has handled it so well, most would say.

While we all do grieve differently, on the outside and on the inside, it did make me wonder if the response and state of mind has more to do with the awareness that the event was coming. Maybe it had more to do with the peace of knowing his passing would be the end of his pain. Or maybe it was more about how she copes with everything as an individual.

Peace and preparation.

So, I asked her. She said there were two contributing factors that helped her move forward without falling apart.

1.   Her child's response to his diagnosis and mortality was one of peace and understanding. He believed that if it was his destiny to die soon that he would go to heaven. Wesley's faith helped grow Angela's faith. It was hard for a time for her to hear that losing her son could be God's will, but Wesley's steadfast hold to Christ strengthened her. Instead of focusing on the despair of losing him, she intended to make as many happy family moments with him as possible in the time they had left, however long that would be. And she did.

2.   She had time to prepare herself for the moment he was gone. This actually reinforces the theory that **while we are not in control of what happens to us, we are in control of how we react.** While my friend, Angela, was given enough time to process and make the end of her son's life one of peace and understanding, there will still always be a void in her life. But she was able to come to terms in a way that accentuated the positives from an otherwise unfathomable negative.

When the time came to make the choice about whether they'd continue treatment, Wesley was able to be a part of that. He was strong and, overall, unquestioning. His faith never wavered and he inspired so many. Even his younger brother gave his life to Christ shortly after Wesley passed because of the impression Wesley's faith left on his heart. **It was a sad loss but one that was soaked in love and growth instead of bitterness, regret, and anger.**

No surprises, please.

Sudden loss alternatively leaves little or no time to process and prepare. I remember reading the horrific Facebook post in morning traffic on the streets of Music City as I made my way to work. I peeked to check for updates on one of my best friends in the whole world. She had just had her third baby and was not doing well. It was scary and I was worried but was so sure she would be fine in no time.

As I opened the app, I couldn't believe what I was reading. My friend was dead. I couldn't breathe. It was like a swift kick in the chest had knocked out all of my breath. I couldn't scream or cry for at least five seconds, and when my breath finally came, it was in a wail of denials.

I pulled over into a gas station, wild with sobs. If anyone passing by had taken a glance at my car they would have had me committed. *No*, it couldn't be true. *No*, not Jules.

How could she be gone? How could everyone live without her? How *could I* live without her? I cried until I had no more tears. I cried until my eyes were so swollen they could barely open and until my body was exhausted. I was sad and I wanted to call her. I wanted to hear her laugh. I wanted her to tell me she was fine.

And y'all, the hurt was so heavy, yet this was only my friend. I think about my friends who have lost a child and how much more terrible that would be.

As much as I loved Julia, the love of a mom for her child is like the most powerful thing in the world. I honestly don't know how my friends who have lost their children, especially suddenly and without warning, don't physically implode. What Angela said to me about having time to process and how that helps, makes perfect sense.

How do you find purpose through the shock? If time is what it takes to heal, how much is enough or how much is too much?

It's different for everyone. *But it's okay to laugh again.* It's okay to be joyful and honor your lost loves by living your life in a way that pleases God. Never forget them, but rejoice in their memory, always recognizing and being grateful for how knowing them has changed who you are. If you heal, peace will come. *Nobody expects you to forget.* I don't want you to forget. **I want you to mend.**

The badder the better...

The second type of grief comes from losing something that was bad for us, something or someone we still know impacts our life negatively but we don't want to give it up. This might be the ending of a bad relationship, one that likely caused pain. Or maybe you're ending an addiction or making any major life change in which you are trading one set of pros and cons for another.

The severity of the grieving depends on one's ability to recognize what good is replacing the bad and how much emotional attachment is still there for the bad despite the logical need for it to go. And of course, physical and psychological addictions and dependency may add a whole extra layer of complication.

Whenever we are in these situations, we might have been holding onto it for so long that we sugarcoat the bad. We can justify the good we get out of it.

So, even if the net result of ridding yourself of the person or activity or thing means you are better off, you'll feel the hole that is left behind.

You must come to terms with the fact that the bad outweighs the good before you can find the will to push it away.

And even then, it is often extremely difficult. There is a chemical and physical connection, a craving, a dependence to the addiction that makes you sick without it. There are many factors that can contribute to the formation of addiction: Genetic predisposition, culture, and exposure to drugs can cause a unique neurological pathway that didn't exist for the user before. The activation of the neurons for someone who is addicted can drive the behavior in an effort to feel normal or at a steady state.

For a relationship, it may be fear of what the change would mean. Sometimes the addiction is physical, emotional, or financial dependence.

For whatever reason, these dependencies throw logic out the window and we lead with our fear and hold on until our knuckles are white. And when it's gone, we should be renewed and happy, yet there can be a sadness for what once was: that feeling the satisfaction of meeting an unhealthy need gave us.

My brother-in-law Justin is sober for almost two years now. For him, the decision to get clean came from the approaching birth of my niece, his first child, and the financial burden of buying pills on the street.

I remember my sister Rachel's strength as she went through her final trimester of pregnancy. She was emotional and tired, yet she took care of the house and their two dogs. She worked full time and made the two-hour trip from Jackson to Nashville at least once a week to spend time with Justin at visitation and family support group or counseling while he was in rehab. I was in awe of her. She had compassion for her husband; she had hope in her heart that this struggle would end in victory. Above all, she knew that to get there, she would have to pull some heavy weight first. She was intent that her baby would come home to a healthy, happy family.

Rachel and I both have the flaw of being a bit impatient when we feel others are not being accountable for their actions or when they are not considering our needs. We have been known to cut people out of our lives. So, I wondered why she had chosen to stay with Justin for so long. He had battled with addiction for at least five years and it had caused problems for them.

From the outside, I would have never guessed. He was so responsible, a college graduate with a well-paying stable job, and seemed confident and together. But on the inside, there was trouble. He felt he needed the pills to be himself. In his words, from his perspective, they brought out the best version of him, and then over time, the "him" started to change as he couldn't be without them and eventually the cost of the addiction became another stressor that was just too much.

Rachel had been in another long-term relationship in the past in which her partner was an alcoholic. He was hurtful to her and never admitted fault, and she didn't put up with that very long. I wanted to know what was different this time. Was it because she just loved Justin so much that she couldn't be without him? Was it the pregnancy that made her stay in even the most stressful of times?

She said it was because she loved him, but also because she believed he wanted to change, and that he was capable. And she was right. When it came to crunch time, he made up his mind. He admitted to his faults and signed up for rehab. It was humble and brave.

He told me about the first day. It was terrifying, he said. He was scared of how he would feel without the drugs. He didn't want to be sick from the detox. He was going to have to sort his feelings and change his way of thinking. Pills were his best friend and worst enemy at the same time. They were his outlet and his strength until they became his poison. Addiction skews your perception, lowers your inhibitions. For Justin, the pills were a means of connection with friends, and eventually they became his identity.

He told us his counselor said, "In order to be sober, the only thing that had to change was everything until he could regain control." It was not easy of course. During detox, he hurt everywhere, so badly he felt he physically could not move. Some of the people he was in rehab with wanted to simmer in those horrible feelings for awhile. They wanted to use them as a deterrent from ever using again, a reminder of how much they had to go through to overcome the grip the drugs had on their body.

Justin, though, wanted to find an alternative to the pain, a distraction that caused positive feelings to reinforce the process: Taking a walk outside, talking to a friend, getting excited about something. He had decided that this was what was best for him and best for his newly growing family. When he came home, the work and healing continued with daily support from his sponsor, weekly group meetings, and continual self-reflection and motivation.

There have been a few times he regretted getting sober because he felt like he was missing out, but he knows clearly what the payoff has been. He feels it has been worth it in every way. He knows there is the chance he could have one beer or maybe two and not risk relapse, but why risk it? If he isn't sure where the slope starts, he would rather just stay on stable ground.

It is essential you fill the inevitable void left behind by the bad thing with peace, love, God, and healthy pleasures. If you know you need to let go of something, make a list of all of the positive things you have not been able to do because of the presence of this thing in your life. Whatever your bad glue is that you have trouble walking away from, when you find the will and strength to do it, the feelings of accomplishment and empowerment and new life will overpower any feeling of loss you may feel.

For Justin, what fills his void are God, baby Eden, a healthy marriage, and mixed martial arts. All of them remind him of his value and give him feelings of accomplishment, connection, and comfort. They give him a sense of control over any temptation or negativity that threatens his sobriety.

Often, our relationships are based on commonalities. As Justin's activities and circumstances started to change, some of the friendships he had during his addiction started to fade away. I asked if this shifting of his circle was painful and if it made him feel abandoned. His answer was insightful and gracious. He said he felt that because they were his friends, they didn't want to put him in an uncomfortable position. But they also knew that they weren't going to change their lifestyle so disconnecting seemed like the logical response. And that didn't hurt his feelings at all.

Some of his life-long friends have found that Justin is now more like the friend they loved before the drugs took over his life. They support him and enjoy connecting with him, even if it were a little awkward at first, and they didn't know what to say to a newly sober Justin. He has new connections with stronger, positive commonalities like parenthood, resilience, and sobriety. These have replaced the relationships that have been lost. And his sponsor and his cousin, who are also recovering addicts, have become a lifeline for him. They are his closest friends and confidants.

I am proud of the growth and progress that he and Rachel have made as a couple. They are good people and good parents. I am proud to call Justin family. I am proud of his faith, humility, and compassion and of the love he has for my sweet little niece. I am proud of the strong woman and loving mother my baby sister has become. I am proud of the choice they have made to work together to live healthy and joyfully while leaning on God.

A few months ago, Justin debuted in his first MMA fight, a Black Tie boxing event. Rachel stood at the side of the ring, looking stunning, but feeling anxious as her eyes twinkled towards this man she had supported through the toughest moments of his life. She was always trying to protect him from pain and now she was about to watch as he put himself in the path of danger as soon as the bell sounded. Friends and family (Tyler and myself were among the crowd in the balcony) were scattered in cheering sections around the Jackson arena shouting encouragement: "LET'S GO J-ROCK! LET'S GO JUSTIN!"

With his sobriety still rather fresh and his mother having passed away just two weeks before the fight, many of us worried about his state of mind leading up to this day. But knowing how far he had come and how hard he had worked to get here cemented our faith. Now, we watched as punches and kicks tore their way through the air, the sound sickening as the blows landed. All attention was focused on the action in the ring, and the excitement was thick and contagious.

The fight lasted all three rounds. It was intense and at the end, the judges' votes were unanimous. *Justin won*! We cheered and yelled with relief, and Rachel cried and laughed as she hugged him. He had overcome so much over the last 18 months. This was not the first fight he had won, it was just the first one in the ring.

As Pink Floyd sings, "Don't look back and lament."

Another version of grief is lament, or regret. This is something we bring onto ourselves and is a common contributor to depression. Some decisions have long-lasting impacts and unexpected or unintended consequences. Sometimes, we can "beat ourselves up" about the what-ifs, even if they aren't realized until years later.

It is done. You can't rewind and change your decision. All you can do is manage what you have at hand and mold the future the best that you can.

Many times, this type of grief can be the most tormenting because it involves self-blame. If you don't actively control it, self-blame can be very destructive of self and of the good things currently happening in your life. If the decisions we regret adversely impacted someone we love, that also adds another layer of negative complexity that is difficult to get past. In a bit, I'll give a personal example. Those of you who may be struggling with this are not alone.

Regret is often its worst under two distinct circumstances.

The first: times when your decision was against your moral compass but **you ignored your conscience** and pushed forth anyway.

These decisions can haunt you forever because you had that gut feeling, be it the conviction of the Holy Spirit and voice inside your head or your conscience. Your moral compass isn't just warning you, it's whaling on your insides, telling you not to be an idiot. But you told it to shut the heck up. The "I told you so's" of these encapsulated friends can be never ceasing when you know they were right and things didn't turn out for the best.

We all have had regrets—*all* of us! Some people may say, "I have *no* regrets! I have learned something from every decision good and bad!"

I don't disagree completely. This whole book, in case you haven't noticed, is about how you control your reactions. It's about how you can in fact make the best of a bad situation even if the bad situation was brought on primarily by the big Y-O-U yourself. But it is only natural to feel guilty or sad when you know that the unpleasant outcomes you are dealing with could have in fact been avoided. I am sure you have a million examples of this one already in your head and I have more than I care to admit, but the *Bible* says we are to live free of condemnation, including the condemnation we inflict on ourselves.

If your heart is feeling convicted, you can find forgiveness and freedom! In the *Bible*, John proclaims, *"My little children, I am writing these things to you so that you may not sin. But if anyone does sin, we have an advocate with the Father, Jesus Christ the righteous"* (1 John 2:1).

And David writes, *"For as high as the heavens are above the Earth, so great is His steadfast love toward those who fear Him; as far as the east is from the west, so far does He remove our transgressions from us"* (Psalm 103:11–12).

The second type: When you can't make amends. When the ship has sailed. When the better-late-than-never opportunity has become nonexistent. When this happens, we have to find a way to mend our hurt and loss without the resolution we feel we needed to heal.

If there is a relationship that you felt ended badly and they pass before you can tell them how you really feel, the heartache of knowing you won't get the opportunity to make it up to them can be unbearable. If it's a family member, never getting to tell them how sorry you are for things that happened, knowing that they'll never understand how you really feel, can feel like an insurmountable loss.

Often, we feel closure is needed in order to forgive ourselves. Other times, maybe you just went too far. You know you will never earn the forgiveness of another person because what you did was so bad. If they could never forgive you, then **how can you forgive yourself?**

To forgive is divine.

I read a moving story online several years ago. It, in fact, can still be found to this day at https://www.littlethings.com/mary-johnson-forgives-murderer and it tells of an amazing lady, Mary Johnson. The author, Emerald Pellot, shares how Mrs. Johnson's 20 year-old-son was murdered by a 16-year-old named Oshea Israel. Israel served 17 years for his crime.

While Mrs. Johnson felt anger and resentment towards this teen for what he had stolen from her, years after he was sentenced, she visited him in prison. Something happened. She no longer saw him in the same light. As they hugged, she changed, she forgave, and they began a new relationship that will last a lifetime: She became his mother figure. And she went on to create From Death To Life, an organization that helps the families of victims of violence to heal and reconcile.

While many of you reading this book may compare your sins against others,

I am sure you will find they pale against murdering someone's child. But atonement was possible for Mr. Israel and forgiveness was possible for Mrs. Johnson.

Was it that bad?

Did you have an affair? Did you gossip, spreading information about someone? Maybe that someone couldn't climb out of the quicksand of their self-deprecation already. Did you take credit for something someone else did? Did you steal? Did you stop calling your best friend because you were envious or maybe because she needed you and you thought her drama was just "too much work" and now you aren't even friends at all?

Just do it.

I challenge you in this moment. I challenge you to forgive yourself. Know that only Jesus had feet that walked on this Earth sin free, fault free, and blameless. Whatever you did is forgiven by Him, and in order for you to convert the negative situation that you created into a positive one where you can still find peace and happiness (even if that person never forgives you) you have to ask God for forgiveness. Then ask the people you've wounded for forgiveness if you can. Then you must forgive yourself.

You made a mistake. Maybe it was a big one. You cannot go back **but you can leave it behind you.**

> *Therefore, if anyone is in Christ, the new creation has come: The old has gone, the new is here! All this is from God, who reconciled us to Himself through Christ and gave us the ministry of reconciliation: that God was reconciling the world to Himself in Christ, not counting people's sins against them. And He has committed to us the message of reconciliation. We are therefore Christ's ambassadors, as though God were making his appeal through us. We implore you on Christ's behalf: Be*

reconciled to God. God made Him who had no sin to be sin for us, so that in Him we might become the righteousness of God.

— 2 Corinthians 5:17–21

See, even the *Bible* says to ask for forgiveness and put it behind you!

No man (or woman) is without sin.

Here is your second challenge: in the same breath, **forgive others who have sinned against you.**

You are new. You are redeemed.

Maybe they didn't ask you for forgiveness. You know what, **maybe they aren't even sorry!** Infuriating, I know. Maybe they aren't even aware of how severely their actions have impacted you. Or maybe they are aware and they just don't care.

So, why should you forgive them?

Because it will heal you. Free yourself of the negativity and the darkness. Push it out of every corner in you. Jesus calls us to forgive others as God forgives us.

It will make you a better person, and you will be astonished at how good it feels!

You wouldn't believe it, but…

My example, for your pleasure:

One time, I got fired!

When you pour your heart and body into what you do, when you think that each task you do each day is to help others, when you try to live each day with the highest integrity, you think something like this could never happen to you. It can threaten your livelihood. The situation is hurtful.

First, let me explain why this impacted me so profoundly and, at the same time, was so ludicrous.

I was well into my career. I thought there would be protection in professionalism once you have a degree. I believed that, in the healthcare profession, "care for others" was the basis for the way that we all practice and treat others. I also believed the system would protect me if I always followed the rules and policies.

I had truly dedicated myself. I worked long hours, even staying at work for nearly three days straight once. I slept on the floor of my office on a blowup bed during an ice storm to ensure my team was supported.

I built positive working relationships between pharmacy and nursing and other departments where they had been lacking and diligently worked in engaging staff to improve the work environment, and in the midst of a leadership change, I was told that I should consider other opportunities should they present. There was a "new sheriff in town." I had seen something like this happen to Billy before and I could see the writing on the wall.

I pride myself on my integrity. Yes, I have made mistakes in the past, but I can't think of even a single lie that I haven't confessed. I am that person who goes back to pay after inadvertently walking out of the store with an unpaid case of water under the buggy. If I think there is even a possibility that I am outside of policy, I always ask my boss or a colleague to ensure my decision is sound.

Also, I found value in hard work early. For me it is fulfilling. Even in college, I took on a double class load one semester while working as a phlebotomist at the hospital. The challenge in the morning, the gratification of a full checklist marked through, and the exhaustion at the end of the day are my drugs.

It is new that I am finding solace in balance instead, but I am still much this way at my core. So, being fired felt like the worst that could happen, professionally.

I truly felt to be the victim of workplace bullying and was continually being written up for fabricated claims. I had never felt this way before. I wasn't a "mean girl" and as an adult, thought that other "mean girls" surely grew out of that mentality. I was anxious every day, worried that this would be the day that my security was ripped away.

We needed my paycheck to survive at the time, and no matter how badly I wanted to leave, I would definitely not quit without having secured another job first. I felt the actions against me were calculated and conniving, and in the end, it was a complete and total lie that sealed the coffin.

Just writing it even years later still makes my cheeks hot I admit so maybe I am not completely healed yet. But I am getting there. I have been surprised to find out that this type of thing has happened to many friends and colleagues. I have found that sharing our experiences with each other has helped us to feel less shame about it. But even now, there are times I worry that someone might judge my ethics and performance from the fact that I got fired, regardless of the circumstances.

Carrying secrets is heavy. With time, I have found freedom in sharing— floating it into the wind.

So how did I find closure?

At first, I felt getting fired in this way was shocking, and that it could happen to absolutely anybody if it could happen to me. After pouring my heart into my work and priding myself on integrity, I felt strangely relieved to be out of that "hell hole" of daily anxiety and insecurity I was in, and I didn't want others to ever have to go through what I was going through.

First, I did what I felt was the strong thing to do, I did a peer review to bring light to what I felt was the injustice of what happened. I got a lawyer and I filed an EEOC claim. It felt like being on trial: I despise ever being put in a position to look like a bad guy or a victim, especially if it's not true, and I was made to look like both at the same time!

How someone treats you says nothing about you and everything about them.

I was warned that these efforts might be fruitless because our state is an at-will employment state, but I knew that **I had done all that I could do** to try and protect others from my fate. I had not just laid down and died in defeat, and I tried to focus on the positives that came from this negative and hurtful event.

Secondly, *I thanked God.*

You might think being grateful for being fired is crazy, but I was in an unhappy predicament. While I didn't pray to be fired, I knew that something major would need to happen for me to be pushed in the right direction. It was really hard to see what that was at the time.

Through tears of course, half grieving, half rejoicing, I praised God **(not prayed, but praised)** for the next opportunity that would be a better opportunity than the one that I had. I thanked him for it before I saw it come to pass. I believed whole heartedly in its existence, confessing complete and total faith.

We would not be able to keep our home or pay our bills or anything without God's provision. While I was at my job, God's provision typically came largely through my employment, so I knew we weren't prepared for me to go months without me working. I didn't know what the answer was, but I also knew that I didn't have to worry.

I took screenshots of these verses on my phone so they were always readily available and quoted them under my breath until they were ingrained into the wrinkles of my brain.

"You intended to harm me, but God intended it for good to accomplish what is now being done…" (Genesis 50:20).

"Therefore I tell you, do not worry about your life, what you will eat or drink; or about your body, what you will wear. Is not life more than food, and the body more than clothes? Look at the birds of the air; they do not sow or reap or store away in barns, and yet your heavenly Father feeds them. Are you not much more valuable than they? Can any one of you by worrying add a single hour to your life? And why do you worry about clothes? See how the flowers of the field grow. They do not labor or spin. Yet I tell you that not even Solomon in all his splendor was dressed like one of these. If that is how God clothes the grass of the field, which is here today and tomorrow is thrown into the fire, will He not much more clothe you-you of little faith? So do not worry, saying, 'What shall we eat?' or 'What shall we drink?' or 'What shall we wear?' For the pagans run after all these things, and your heavenly Father knows that you need them. But seek first His kingdom and His righteousness, and all these things will be given to you as well. Therefore do not worry about tomorrow, for tomorrow will worry about itself. Each day has enough trouble of its own" (Matthew 6:25–34).

I am redeemed.

I am happy to report it was only seven days before I had another job, and not just another but a better job. It was a job that was absolutely perfect for me and my experience and my abilities and my desire to grow. My new employer enthusiastically accepted all of me, even though I was upfront regarding what had happened at my previous employment. I was a little nervous that

I would be suddenly blacklisted from all other desirable teams. But this was a better opportunity. In it, I thrived and had the ability to improve processes and patient care. I loved my team there and it was a place that was exactly what I needed and when I needed it.

God also blessed me in other ways that month, too, to remind me that **He is my Father, my provider, and loves me.**

I was able to spend a week off with the boys on their spring break, and we spent time with friends and family and quality time at my grandmother's, which still feels like a secret place of safety that never seems to change. And then I received a call from an old employer: They had found unreconciled paid time off and sent me a check for it! It meant I made more money that month than if I had worked.

I took time to reconnect with friends I had been neglecting because I had been miserable and unfriendly until my departure.

And, I started this book.

We are all human, after all.

I could hate the person I felt was responsible for my termination. I felt that person put their own interests and feelings ahead of anything else. Their actions could have hurt my family and our well-being. In my story, I saw this person's intention was to tear me down.

I have forgiven. It was hard. They didn't ask for it. They probably don't want it or care to have it. I don't know if they are sorry, and I suppose that maybe they aren't. I didn't forgive them because it was asked. I forgave because I don't want feelings of resentment or hate to cloud my judgment or shadow my goals. I forgave because Jesus forgave me before I even asked.

I wondered what the encounter would be like if I ever ran into this person again. After all, being in our profession, I assumed it would happen eventually. I wondered how I could possibly be amicable. Well, it happened a little over three years later, and I was surprisingly unaffected. It was not like a scene from *Ally McBeal* where Ally pictures herself flying through the air across tables to attack. It was completely and utterly uneventful, as you might have expected. There was a surprised, "Oh, hi" from each of us, and that was it.

No, this is not a story that ends by me telling you that we are now the best of friends and spend every weekend on the lake together with the husbands and kids. I would be lying if I said I wanted that.

I will be content if we never make amends, but I can honestly say that I am mended because I forgave.

I recognize that despite what might have been their ill intention, I have been able to use what happened to learn about myself, to grow my faith, to learn new things, to meet new people and friends, to push myself and grow my dreams. I can still know that what happened to me was wrong and unfair, but I also know that a **bad break does not mean defeat**.

And remember, sometimes the story isn't always about you. Maybe I was an innocent bystander in a story that wasn't about me, and maybe this person is not the person I remember. Maybe it was out of character and just part of God's plan, but regardless, harboring hurt really only hurts you. So, you owe it yourself to free yourself.

Finding purpose in your pain.

And my last challenge for you, regardless of which type of grief you are suffering, is to turn your loss into a new beginning that will help others.

Think of burying this grief like burying a seed, not a corpse. Let it flower into something beautiful.

Mrs. Johnson started From Death to Life. My friend Angela has started a foundation in Wesley's name, the Wesley's Warriors Foundation, to help families meet their basic needs and still be able to take time off when their children are battling cancer. And I try to be a dedicated advocate of other parents of kids with amputations and with cancer. I share resources for their kids to connect with others, try new things, and reach for their dreams. I joined the board of a charity organization that helped me do that, became involved in other adaptive organizations, volunteered with Make-A-Wish and am constantly looking for other ways to serve. I wrote this book, which I hope will help you and others find faith in God and the strength within themselves.

You are made uniquely. You have abilities that are special and fantastic. You might have talents that are still yet to be uncovered.

Think about what you needed when you were needy or in a hard place.

How can you now meet that need for someone else?

It may seem impossible, but water your dream. Grow it, talk about it, research resources, and put a little time into it every day, even if it's just 10 minutes and all you do is take mental notes on your progress and next steps. Envision what the accomplishment will look like when it's come to fruition.

Sometimes connections and courage will even come from unexpected places as God nourishes your mental commitment.

It might come from someone sitting beside you on an airplane, or your neighbor, or maybe even a complete stranger. Maybe you'll inspire them by being vocal and open. I met one of my dearest friends, who lives in another country, when she struck up a conversation with me on a hotel elevator in a city located halfway between us! I believe this was not merely coincidence and she has been instrumental to me in this process of sharing my story with you.

Last but not least.

The last form of grief I'll discuss is empathic grief.

This is a genuine grief knowing someone else is feeling loss.

I am in awe of those in careers that involve helping others deal with major loss, like law enforcement officers, social workers, healthcare providers, and those in ministry. These people can be genuinely empathic, and also strong and calm and objective to help those people who are going through grief.

I grieved empathically for Angela. I didn't know exactly what the loss felt like but I knew the love she had for Wesley. I knew how terrifying it was to fear losing Tyler. I wanted to bear some of her burden as her friend and as a mother who had been scarred from the battle with childhood cancer. I wanted to wrap her with a blanket of God's peace. I wrote the following passage for her and sent it in an email on the morning after Wesley's death.

"It rained all day yesterday with an unshakable chill. It was like the world was sad.

I woke up this morning to slurry white snow. It was the first day into Daylight Saving so it was dark dreary still. And I wondered . . . I wondered what it must be like to wake up as her today. To wake up and know that this was the first day of many in a world without him. A world that now had a void bigger than the ocean could fill. She must wonder how she could have been so lucky to have been his mother. What would she miss the most? Would it be his kind sparkling eyes? Would it be that great big smile? Would it be his contagious laugh or warm bear hugs? She must wonder how God could create someone so special and so amazing from her very being. She must wonder how many lives he touched during his short time on Earth and how many people missed out on the special chance to get to know him?

I imagine that her arms and ears and eyes must miss him

already. How did the time go by so fast? If only we knew how many moments we would get with the ones we love, would it change how we would spend them? Would we speak softer, would we live bolder, would we be more grateful, or would we resent the clock for ticking too fast? This special child knew that the next life was welcoming and pain free, was timeless and the sun would always shine. There would be no more medicine or needles or symptoms. No crime or cruelty. No worry at all. There would be love and only love. He would not miss his family because for him they would be home with him soon. But she, left behind with his memory still fresh, his smell still on her clothes, she must find strength in the savior that lived in her son's big warm heart. It would be him that would give her peace and calm her spirit and hold her hand when it is empty. She must remember that she has a job left to do. An important and rewarding job. She gets to be the neck for four more sweet little arms to hug and 20 more fingers that need to be held and four more cheeks to kiss goodnight. She has to be the cheerleader at their games and help them with homework and teach them to drive. She needs to race them in the backyard and tie their neck ties before their proms . . . and graduations . . . and weddings. If God allows the time, she needs to change diapers for her grandbabies and hold her husband's hand whenever he needs her strength and love.

Those around her will awe at her grace, at her wisdom, at her stripes that have come hard earned. She will teach them about God's grace and love and forgiveness. Knowing him made her a better person and missing him will draw her closer to heaven.

Also, in case you forget, you did good sister . . . raising him, being strong for him, doing what you had to do, you did good, the whole thing!!!!"

Grief unfolding.

Granted, I am not a psychologist or renowned expert on the topic, but from my experience as a watcher, I think that the Kübler-Ross model, which chronicles the progression through the stages of grief after a terminal illness, is quite accurate. Depending on the way that the loss occurs, and certain characteristics about the person and, many times, the circumstances allowing grief will dictate the length that someone will stay in each stage.

According to the Kübler-Ross model, we grieve in the following five stages: denial, anger, bargaining, depression, and acceptance.

The stages might be set, but you do you.

It's okay to respond to grief in your own way. Take as much time as you need in each stage, but make sure you continue to move through the stages toward resolution. We can't anticipate what we may respond to if we were in that situations, but I encourage you to explore the resources that might help you progress towards acceptance and emotional healing.

You might need a change in the environment or you might need familiarity. There are church groups and support groups dedicated to grief. There are counselors and grief centers. And I bet your friends who offered a shoulder back when you didn't feel like you needed it are still waiting in the wings for you to reach out. Don't be too proud. Getting the help you need is not admitting weaknesses, it's being resourceful and taking action.

Most importantly, don't judge others that are dealing with grief. Even if you feel you've been in their shoes, that doesn't mean you know what's best for them.

I know that seems like a given. I can hear your brain right now, "Judge? Me? No, never!" But people often do it without even realizing it.

Maybe you've overheard something like this:

"You know, I saw Jane at the store the other day. She looked a wreck, bless her heart. No makeup, jogging pants, hair just a mess! I mean, I know she has been so sad since her husband died but it has been a *whole* year, and you know being sad is not going to bring him back. Maybe she should think about getting out and meeting people. Maybe I can talk to her sister about getting her on a dating website, it worked for my cousin . . . "

So on and so on. I know you've heard it before!

Without even realizing, we often assume we know what is best for someone else. But everyone heals in their own time.

I encourage you to be an empathetic griever. Try to understand what stage your friend, colleague, or family member might be in. Offer comfort where you can. It is easy to feel overwhelmed and unsure of what to do because you can't fix their situation, so you abandon them. Maybe they seem like they don't want or need you around, and maybe they don't....in that stage. But maybe they do. Maybe they will. Your job is to continue to let them know that you are there for them, even when they don't need you yet.

And realize that for some, finding joy in remembering is the real healing, not forgetting. So, help them remember if that's what they need!

Realize that they at some point will want or need some normalcy. They will need to laugh again. They will need to love again.

Be a friend that adapts to their stage. And be patient. You might gain something on the other side that you never knew you needed.

Roll Call

HOW SHOWING UP FOR OURSELVES AND OTHERS CAN HELP US HEAL

If a tree falls in the forest, but no one is there to hear it, does it make a sound?

Who cares? I think the real question here is, "Where was everybody?"

So, attention.

Attention please.

Are y'all out there still listening and ready?

Have you ever heard that half the battle is just showing up? We must decide again and again whether or not we show up.

Every action we take or don't take is a decision.

To this point, I hope you've learned a lot about slaying your adversity.

We've established:

- Why you are reading this,
- How to be strong: It helps to know who we are and where we came from,
- That bad things happen to everybody,
- How we can control our actions so that life isn't just about surviving; it's about coming out better than before,
- That desperate times call for desperate measures. It's better to have a plan ahead of time,
- That we are not alone,
- That maybe it's not about us, and
- That it's okay to grieve, in our own way and at our own pace. Our actions and attitude can ensure it won't last forever.

So, now let's talk about how showing up for ourselves and others can help us heal.

If you agree with Pink Floyd, maybe you won't be there for roll call. Why would you show up and possibly learn something if you think you "don't need no education."

But if you're here, and you're still listening, follow me. Choosing to be here is a choice.

Not choosing is still a choice!

Newton's law is that for every action, there is an equal and opposite reaction.

When you decide even the smallest thing, you are making a decision not to do something else. **The choice may seem small, but what about its ripple effect?**

Let's say you choose to stay in bed today. What are you saying yes to? You are saying yes to rest and no to work. You are choosing to not be present one place to "show up" for something else: a little rest and relaxation.

You are weighing the risks and benefits. It doesn't mean you will make a choice in which the benefits outweigh the risks, but even in the decision not to act, you are still making a choice. You are still saying yes to something.

I like sleep. I also like kickboxing and Zumba. But sometimes—lots of times—I say yes to sleep and no to an early morning workout.

I know that while rest is important, I have probably had enough, and saying no to sleep would be more productive, more effective. By showing up for sleep, I am bailing on the workout, on maybe running the vacuum before hopping on my laptop, saying no to cooking an elaborate breakfast, or doing some meditation or something else that might be more beneficial to me than 30 more minutes of sleep.

The second-place winner is the first-place loser when it comes to choices.

I want you to soak this in for a moment. Saying yes to one thing is saying no to something else, and much of the time, half the battle is just showing up. And when we don't show up, who will be the one to suffer?

After going to many practices, games, and meets including but not limited to baseball, wrestling, cross country, track, wheelchair basketball, and soccer to be the mom on the sidelines, I realized something.

The kids don't care if I go and scream my heart out. Actually, I'm confident that they prefer it when I don't cheer. Peyton gets embarrassed and Tyler said I sound like a 12-year-old girl. But they still care that I show up.

And they care whether or not I pay attention, but half the battle is just showing up.

When you don't show up, who really suffers?

I have been blessed to be in a management or leadership role for essentially my entire adult life. And even though the emotional impacts of presence aren't as profound in the workplace, even here it serves a fundamental purpose. My advice on day one is always: I need you to know how important it is for you to be here.

You can't learn if you're not here.

You can't help if you're not here.

Even if you showed up and did absolutely the minimum necessary, you have still been better for your team than your absence would have been. And you are less likely to be asked not to come back the more you actually show up for your responsibility regardless of what that is (job, team practice, relationship, etc.).

Half the battle is just showing up. And if you don't show up, everyone else suffers, too—maybe even more than you.

And now what...

Every place we go, every choice we make, has a purpose. And now that you're here, you may as well do something!

Sometimes we don't know what it is when we get there, but there is a purpose. If you go to a movie, the purpose is to be entertained. Go to the doctor to get better. Stay home to relax or work or clean, but there is a purpose.

You are here to do something.

Even more, you were *born* to do something. Some of us were born to do lots of things. Lanco sings a song about being born to love (I saw them in concert, and they were phenomenal). Many of us find what we feel we were just "born to do" changes with age and experience, but I believe we all have purpose.

And first and foremost, we have to show up. I believe God has a plan for our lives, but we also have to put forth effort.

♪♪ *"If you wanna be somebody, if you wanna go somewhere, you better wake up and pay attention."* ♪♪

♪♪ *"If you wanna be somebody, if you wanna go somewhere, you better wake up and pay attention."* ♪♪

I wish every version of this book had an audio component. I am one of those people who constantly, and I mean constantly, has a song in her head. Many times, the soundtrack is meaningless, like a song played 8.2 million times per week on the radio. That song is usually absolutely annoying, and that's why it's ingrained in my cerebellum. Other times, the song in my head is a reflection of my entire state of being at the moment.

I have my individual playlists for when I'm in my feels or feeling sexy. Stone Temple Pilots or Mazzy Star when I'm melancholy. A little gangster rap or my favorite country song when I'm sassy. But then sometimes, music is my remedy. It's the way that my heart rejoices. It's how I'm inspired. It's how I worship with my soul. I don't even have to sing out loud (although I often do) for it to truly have an impact on me or put me in a new frame of mind. In keeping with being grateful, I am constantly grateful for my ability to hear.

The above little ditty is from a movie that I recommend every human see at least once in their lifetime, *Sister Act 2: Back in the Habit*. Now let me tell you that growing up, my watchlist was severely limited. Until at least the age of 16, I was only able to watch movies that were rated G, PG, or in some cases (if prescreened and void of sexual conduct and foul language) PG-13.

So many of the movies I saw were either replayed many times or were the ones edited for TV and appropriate for a general viewing audience.

This was one of the ones on the approved list. Without being a total spoiler, I'll give you the gist of the storyline for the original *Sister Act*, since you can never really understand a sequel without seeing the first movie.

Whoopi Goldberg plays a Vegas lounge singer who witnesses a crime committed by her bad guy, Mafioso-type boyfriend. She's understandably fearful of him, so she runs away or is put in the witness protection program, or something to that effect and ends up at a convent with a choir of singing nuns.

In part two, Whoopi's character is no longer a nun. But the Catholic school run by the convent is in dire trouble. The nuns call Whoopi in for backup, and she becomes the new music teacher. Of course, the kids in the movie present as an unruly crew completely uninterested in their new teacher or doing classwork, and she has to get them motivated.

She begins to unmask their hidden and very real talent (cue Lauryn Hill) by engaging them in this song, and honestly how can you not be inspired when you hear Lauryn Hill?

♪♪ *"If you wanna be somebody, if you wanna go somewhere, you better wake up and pay attention.* ♪♪

♪♪ *If you wanna be somebody, if you wanna go somewhere, you better wake up and pay attention."* ♪♪

Y'all, it's a beautiful thing to see a person begin to believe in themselves, begin to believe they are capable of more, begin to see possibilities beyond just what they see immediately around them.

It happens right on-screen in *Sister Act 2: Back in the Habit*. And that's why

I think everyone should see this movie. Also, the grand performance at the end is totally joyful.

Tyler believes that he is here with his challenges and his history because he has a purpose. He believes in showing up for that purpose. He wants to be an inspiration to other kids who have struggled with disability. He has to work hard for his grades, but he wants to be an oncologist to devote his life to saving kids like him. He is intent on encouraging others to live a life full of hope. Even at 17, he is working on his own brand of apparel to inspire others to have faith and strength.

Maybe it is a little unrealistic or too good to be true to think that a profound change in your state of mind can happen in a moment or that a song can change your life. **But I believe that a decision is made in a moment.** You may be analytical like me and have to push yourself not to agonize for hours, days, or years over one decision, but when you do make that decision, it happens in a moment.

So yes, I do believe that you can change your life in one instant. **It all starts with a choice.**

Don't just be here, but **BE HERE.**

Half the battle is showing up. Since you are here, live with purpose. Wake up and pay attention.

My kids notice if I'm on my phone when they are practicing soccer. My kids hate it if I talk on the phone after I pick them up. They can see I'm not paying attention.

Even if it seems like nothing is happening, there is always the possibility that something *will* happen. What if they want to share something, what if I missed a moment? You better wake up and pay attention.

People always said, "Don't blink. They grow up so fast." As I write this, my kids are seven, 13, and 17, and this year I realized, oh my goodness, all those people were right.

I have caught my breath at the thought that the days are numbered when my whole family will sleep under this same roof every night. I have wondered, how many moments did I miss while I was striving hard to be the best at everything? How many wrestling matches or soccer practices? How many dinners around the table?

I had been feeling, for the last couple of years, that my priorities had started to weigh too heavy to one side. I was feeling busy and fulfilled at work, even overwhelmed sometimes, but I thought to myself, this is what I have been working towards, right? Being able to invest in my team and in patient care.

My heart had been feeling heavy about missed moments, as I seemed to be spending more time in traffic than I was with my boys, and I began praying that God would help me—with fulfillment, with being in line with his will, with being a mom that the boys will remember as working towards my goals, sure, but mainly, as a mom who was there for them.

Billy was working full time, too, but I began to notice that he was making dinner more than I was. Between him and the kids, I couldn't remember the last time I had done a load of laundry. I believe a family should be a team, and I appreciated them so much, but I started to feel like I wasn't pulling my weight for them in the ways that I wanted to.

If my feelings of guilt and dissatisfaction were trying to tell me that I needed to make some changes, I honestly didn't know how to even start. I began to pray that God would help me see, lead my heart, and open opportunities for me to realign.

The moment of truth was on a Valentine's Day. Easton, my youngest son, was in kindergarten. When your littlest one goes to big-boy school and you have no babies left in the house, it pushes a pressure point. It reminds you how quickly life goes by and looking at my middle schooler and high-school sophomore, I didn't want to miss any more special moments in their lives. But really, what could I do about it?

On this day, I was taking Easton to school. I was supposed to attend the quarterly institutional leadership meeting that morning. I never missed these. They included important updates and goals and were always motivational. I loved these meetings. They reminded me how fortunate I was to be in a position to lead, that it was a special responsibility. But as I pulled into the school parking lot, Easton asked if I were going to stay and help with class Valentine's Day crafts. His teacher had asked for parent volunteers that day, and I had not responded.

It was almost three-quarters through the school year and I had not helped once. I had not even attended a fieldtrip. I couldn't remember how long it had been since I had done this for the other boys either. Two years maybe? I texted my boss to tell her I would be late that day.

I felt a tinge of guilt, but as I walked across the parking lot towards the school holding Easton's little hand, he looked up and grinned at me. So, I made it a point to be completely present for him for the next two hours. My phone stayed in my pocket while I painted a class full of little hands and helped them stamp Valentine's Day poems. I listened to their stories. I helped them read their Valentine's cards from their friends. And I helped wash the red paint off their fingers after they painted messy red hearts on canvas. When the last craft was laid in a row to dry, I hugged Easton and kissed his face and left his class to head to work.

As soon as I got into the car, I started to cry. I had somehow forgotten how important these moments were. When did that happen? When did my drive for accomplishment become so skewed? I felt I was a positive impact to my team and to patient care but at what expense?

I didn't know how to draw a line in the sand. How much good was good enough?

That morning, I felt like I had gotten the chance to share in a special secret, and now I couldn't forget it. I felt an ache to have more of these moments and I felt guilty that I had forgotten to prioritize.

After that day with Easton and his kindergarten class, I truly began to open my heart to the opportunity for change. I began to yearn for more "mom moments." I wanted to eat lunch with them at the special table in the cafeteria reserved for when you have visitors and be home when they got off the school bus. I wanted to be the one that took them to practice and help them with their homework.

So, I prayed for God to give me direction and to either change things right where I was or to lead me to the place that I needed to go. It only took three months, and God brought that change in a new opportunity.

I believe you can make time for many things and you don't have to sacrifice family for work or work for family, but I have worked diligently to whittle down my list of to-dos to only those that are most important to me right now. I have become deliberate and a bit more selfish with my "Yes."

I remind myself that if I'm blessed, when some things come off this list because it's time or even not by my choice, then I can add other things from the wait list to the to-do list. I strive for the balance instead of trying to rise to the top.

What are the things that make you sick to think you missed? What are the fleeting moments that you can't get back?

Those are things you decide to show up for, and you be awake, and you pay attention.

That is how you get to where you need to go. That is how you know what comes next.

Moments are fleeting.

I'm going to mention something again that crosses all boundaries of this book...Regret.

Regret is probably one of the worst poisons.

On the bright side, it's the one danger we have control over. It's one of the hardest feelings to shake because it only affects us at first. Regret can become self-loathing. It can become anxiety. It can grow into depression. And then it starts to seep out to poison everything we love and tarnish everything we try to do. How sad to battle regret from knowing you have missed a moment when you only needed to show up and pay attention! **You don't need any special skill to just do that!**

If it's really important to you, you show up.

It's up to you. **We prioritize what our heart wants.**

Make a conscious decision to get your whole body on the same page. If your heart wants what your mind has already decided is bad for you, work to fill your heart with something new. Sing a new song. Your body will follow where your heart and mind lead. Show up at the right place.

Show up in a way that you can live without regret. And when you get there, pay attention.

Today, the finger-painted red heart Easton and I made together has a permanent place. It is proudly displayed beside my toothbrush (and on the cover of this book) to remind me every morning of the important responsibility God has graced me with. While I have spent my career learning to be a good leader, I have to remember that the three most important minds to mold are right under my own roof. And although I still am thankful for such a fulfilling career and the honor of contributing in even a small way to the fight against cancer and for better patient care, I know that my job as a mom must come first.

I must live with grace and humility, a grateful heart and positive outlook, and a "can do" attitude in the eyes of these impressionable young men, but most importantly, I must be present and teach them about the importance of having a personal relationship with God.

Do-overs are a rarity.

There was a time I did *not* show up for what was important.

Let me confess to you about the time I was a bad friend. I don't think I've shared this before with anyone. I am both embarrassed and saddened by my choice on this occasion *not* to show up.

If you are lucky, you will get to have a few friends in your life who rely on you and want you by their side. I had a friend who was a brief friend. She thought that I was a good friend, a reliable friend, and I believe at first, I was!

We weren't the closest companions, but we were friends. She was younger than me by maybe 10 years, and I knew her from church. She was bubbly and fun. When she and her first husband separated, I was there for her during the separation and divorce, and finding confidence to live on her own. I was happy to be a shoulder to lean on and truly enjoyed our friendship. But as my own busy life prevailed, and as she needed my shoulder less, we started to grow apart. Eventually over the next year, we didn't talk much, and she became blessed with a new man in her life who made her his world.

Although I hadn't become part of her newfound environment yet, she appreciated my friendship and those times I *had* been there for her, and when he proposed, I was one of the lucky few who got the invitation to serve as a bridesmaid.

I said, "Yes."

For every southern gal, this is one of the highest honors one can have bestowed on us, and one I have only been blessed with a couple of times. I should have cried with happiness to be able to be there to stand by my friend and support and love her. **But I didn't do that.**

And what I didn't say to her but should have was that I was going through a really difficult time. Our family had been through some unfortunate events and we had just moved. We were all very stressed in general that maybe we were not where God wanted us to be and feeling unsure of the future. I was in a brand-new job, still in orientation as the wedding neared.

I only said what I always said when I felt someone needed me: "Of course I will!" Despite knowing I was personally overwhelmed, I accepted her invitation hoping I could get myself together, but I didn't. I did the worst thing imaginable.

I had said "Yes." But then the day before her wedding, I bailed! It makes me nauseous to relive this. I know that saying I would be there for her and then not showing up was infinitely more disappointing and hurtful than just being honest with her in the beginning and declining when she asked. I should have known she would have been understanding and would have been there for me.

So, I ended up punishing both of us.

I am sorry.

I definitely don't expect a second chance and I have no idea even of where she is now or how to reconnect after all these years, but if you are out there and you ever read this, from the bottom of my soul I am sorry. I am sure you are living your best life with a wonderful husband and lots of friends. I hope you have a house full of adorable babies and if you ever would be gracious enough to forgive me, I promise to be unfailing and stellar and your most dependable friend until death.

I cross my heart and not merely because my record is blemished. I cross my heart because I am sad at the loss of your friendship and of you in my life and am ashamed I let you down. I let me down, too.

It's our job.

The *Bible* speaks of the value of being there for each other.

"*Two are better than one; because they have a good reward for their labour. For if they fall, the one will lift up his fellow: but woe to him that is alone when he falleth; for he hath not another to help him up*" (Ecclesiastes 4:9–10).

As a friend **it is our duty** to show up. And when we don't? Others suffer. We suffer. And when we know we are not in a position to be what they need, then we must be honest, show we are vulnerable and human, and let them be there for us.

And then, what about when we aren't honest, when we don't show up, when we disappoint and hurt those who rely on us? Well, then we need to find resolve, we need to make amends and move forward. **We cannot be our best self if we are living under a haze of guilt.** God's word proclaims we are free from condemnation, including our own, when we repent.

And what about when people aren't open to forgiveness? What if they move on, move away, or are just too hurt to even hear you? What then?

It's more than the Golden Rule—*doing unto others as you would have them do to you*. Repent, forgive yourself, and show up for yourself and everyone else who loves you and relies on you. Become the friend you should have been, the friend you would want to have, and forgive yourself.

Only you get to decide your next move.

You've all heard the old saying, "When a door closes, a window will open."

Sometimes the opportunities we have to choose from may not be the ones we wanted or the ones we **planned.**

If we feel like the item we wanted is not on the menu, it's easy to say, "This is not my choice, it's not what I wanted."

But I have news for you: *you* **still make the choice.**

To you it may just be picking the better of two evils, or a subpar option, or choosing nothing at all—but you still get to choose.

And if you really, really aren't happy with your options, you can still step outside of your line of vision and figure out how you can create new choices.

Unlike a frame-locked puzzle in which the pieces only slide, you can add options to the equation. What else can you change to get another possible result? Do you need to go back to school? Do you need to make a change in your budget so you can quit that part-time job to have more time to pursue a passion? Do you need to get a part-time job so you have the money to pursue a passion? Do you need to ask for help from friends or family to help you open up another option or help you make an important connection that will lead to opportunity? **Think outside that square.**

The next move is always your move. Be confident in your exploration and humble enough to ask for help, for an outside perspective. Have faith and listen for God to guide you. Know that if you are pursuing a path he has laid on your heart, sometimes he will make a way, even when it seems impossible. When a door closes, maybe you can open up another window on your own or **maybe you figure out how to get that key.**

Show up, wake up, pay attention, and know the next move belongs to you. Half the battle is just showing up, and then pour your heart out and into it.

How will you make them feel?

Let me tell you what it feels like to be on the receiving end when someone shows up.

Just before Tyler's third birthday, we were granted a wish by the Make-A-Wish Foundation.

There is no possible way to verbalize what this experience has meant to us. It would be impossible to recognize everyone that was involved. It took a community to come together for something this special. First, the very busy main road in the city of Southaven was blocked off to accommodate the festivities. Next, a parade started from the fire department. Tyler and Billy sat in the front seat of the big red fire engine and we rode in this parade that was all for Tyler down the street over to the Desoto Athletic Center, the local gym we belonged to.

Police cars with flashing lights accompanied us. Not just one but three of the local high school bands learned songs specifically chosen for the event. They all marched proudly down the street along with our fire engine.

When we arrived at the gym, one of Billy's fellow officers, dressed in a Spiderman uniform, rappelled from 10 stories, from the raised bucket of the fire truck! Spiderman was Tyler's hero and you could tell by the look on his face that he was beyond elated. When Richard came over in costume to give Tyler a big high five, Tyler gave him a gigantic bear hug instead.

For all intents and purposes, Spiderman really was a superhero that day. **It was an *unforgettable* moment.**

And then, Mickey Mouse (who was actually the city alderman in costume) came over to tell Tyler the big news about his birthday trip to Disney World and Universal Studios.

Then we were met with hugs and smiles from what seemed to be the whole town. The high school bands gave Tyler honorary school gear and signed drum tops.

Then we went inside to share celebratory cake with family and friends. The local papers and news channels caught everything, and Tyler's adorable dimpled smile got to shine some positivity into the greater Memphis area homes that night and the next couple of days.

Robert, the owner at the Desoto Athletic Center (the DAC) who made the donation to grant our wish, the staff of Make-A-Wish, the police department, the fire department, the local schools, our church, the members of the community that came to support us, family, and friends: they all "showed up."

And because our community showed up, I will *always* give freely to others of my talent and my time and my effort.

Having Tyler's wish granted changed me, and I am confident that nothing I could ever do could be quite that special, but knowing what the possibilities are sure does keep me motivated to keep trying!

The generosity proved to be contagious. From that experience, Fishes for Wishes, an annual fundraiser for Make-A-Wish, was born. Certain members of the police administration with big hearts were inspired to ensure more little boys and little girls with cancer or chronic illness could also get special moments like we had. Captain Cox, the originator of the effort, has now passed, but Tyler became an extra twinkle in his eye.

Once you see how good it feels to show up, it's almost hard to stop.

If not for you, if not for them, start for Christ.

Work like you're working for Christ and not man.

"Whatever you do, work at it with all your heart, as working for the Lord, not for human masters, since you know that you will receive an inheritance from the Lord as a reward. It is the Lord Christ you are serving" (Colossians 3:23–24).

Live with purpose, with passion, with pleasure in your abilities to "do."

It will be rewarding and fulfilling. It will impact everyone around you, and you will be exhausted.

And, I would wager that at the end of the day you will rest in a way you never have: with peace and resolve, with a feeling of renewal, and with wonder and anticipation of another fulfilling and beautiful day.

Be prayerful and purposeful with the generosity of your time and talent.

What can you do tomorrow? Who can you be? Who can you help?

Even if your track record is bad and you have a lot of absences on your list, even if they won't forgive you, you can forgive yourself, and show up tomorrow and do better, for yourself and others.

You might just be able to give a glimpse of the love of Christ to someone else, inspiring them to give freely, too. The ripple effect of paying it forward might just go on well past what we will ever know or could even comprehend, *all because you showed up.*

Let's Be Real

WHO ARE YOU ANYWAY?

If you are going to show up for yourself and for others, it feels good to be able to present the real you—no apologies, no pretenses. Just you, being the best you that you can be, the you that you feel God has made you to be. And how can we do that? How can we let our guard down? How can we fix us or ask God to, if we don't know what's broken?

Let's be real here. How can we heal when we are pressured to pretend to be okay?

We feel the need to wear a cloak of positivity because being raw makes us feel vulnerable and we fear being exposed makes others uncomfortable. Carrying the weight of this facade can be utterly exhausting, especially in our times of struggle.

If we are too afraid to show who we are to others (or ourselves), then it will deter us from showing up. And if we won't show those around us the authentic version of us, we can't whine about not being accepted. You must always **love the whole you**, even if you don't love all the pieces, even if the pieces are broken.

The purge.

Can you remember the last time you cried?

Was it a quiet, reserved cry when you thought of someone you haven't seen in a long time? Tears that you could barely feel trickling down your face. Your breathing stayed deep, your heart rate steady.

Or were they tears of joy at the sight of a new baby or a long-lost friend? The tears welled, your heart was excited, and your soul wasn't sure if it should be laughing, but instead what came out was a small happy sob.

Were your tears from fear and despair? Was your heart heavy and aching from worry? Maybe your heart was beating fast, your head aching and spinning. Maybe your insides felt laid open to the heavens, begging to be rescued.

Were your cries in anger? Did you feel betrayed by someone, someone whose actions caused hot tears to cover your cheeks with the fury trying to escape you, overflowing the only way it could?

Did you cry tears of humility? Feeling inadequate and undeserving, adoration with a lack of understanding but thankful for a gift of kindness or love bestowed upon you? Tears that each represent a sentiment of thanks that you know you could never verbalize in volume equal to the way that you felt?

Did you hide your tears, releasing them only when no one could see, throw them like darts at your offender, or offer them up to God as a sacrifice?

Did they make you feel exhausted and broken, or clean and renewed?

Are you someone who wears your tears boldly on your sleeve and embraces them when they come? Or do you shield your true feelings and regard your tears as private and shameful, moments that should be hidden as symbols that could be misinterpreted?

Being numb is not normal; it means something is broken. We were *created* to feel.

I used to think my tears were a sign of weakness. I thought crying meant I was losing control. I thought being vulnerable was atrocious.

We were created to express, not suppress.

To teach this, I will admit I was once the student. I felt my tears were a symbol of weakness regardless of their meaning. To have that type of release or response meant I'd lost control, that I was vulnerable. Unacceptable!

As I grow, I realize instead how beautiful tears are.

The fire down below.

(This is not where we talk about STDs—although those could also make someone cry.)

Do you know that forest fires are a natural part of the life cycle of a forest? If you look at the raging flame and destruction of a fire, it seems utterly impossible that good could come of it. Fire takes everything under the canopy in its mouth and swallows it up in an untouchable blaze. It can kill people, wildlife, trees, and bushes.

But the forest also *needs* the fire.

What if there were never fire?

Life would carry on in the forest, safe and happy, right? Well—not exactly.

In a forest's undergrowth, bushes, ground cover, and saplings grow out of control. They fight for water and sunlight. They crowd each other and over-run the lay of the land. They smother the roots of the big trees, preventing them from thriving and growing.

Fire is nature's way of cleaning house and repairing the damage the clutter in the undergrowth has caused.

Our feelings can smother us. Reacting to them, releasing them, is like that forest fire, burning up that undergrowth so that our trees can grow again.

Reserving your tears may mean your eventual release is more meaningful and impactful. Maybe they'll be more *effective* tears. But don't deny yourself the ability to feel for fear of vulnerability.

My dear, it makes you human.

This emotional purge is the cleaning out of the underbrush of anxiety and tension that builds in every nerve.

I didn't say it is easy.

It feels counterintuitive to think vulnerability and strength should coexist in the same being.

But even Jesus showed emotion that indicated he was feeling overwhelmed. *"Then Jesus went with his disciples to a place called Gethsemane, and he said to them, 'Sit here while I go over there and pray.' He took Peter and the two sons of Zebedee along with him, and he began to be sorrowful and troubled. Then he said to them, 'My soul is overwhelmed with sorrow to the point of death. Stay here and keep watch with me.' Going a little farther, he fell with his face to the ground and prayed, 'My Father, if it is possible, may this cup be taken from me. Yet not as I will, but as you will'"* (Matthew 26:36–39).

I struggle with this still.

My mother is a free crier. She literally cries at everything. Happy, sad, worried, mad. I joke with her it's as common for her as a laugh or smile. I used to judge her, now I don't. I used to think she must be weak, now I think she's brave for allowing herself to feel whatever her soul wants.

When I shared with her that I was pregnant, she cried. Not just the first time, all three times! The first time, I was young and in college, and she was scared what it might mean for my future, so I get it. The second time, I was in pharmacy school, and maybe she was concerned that pregnancy would mean too much added stress, along with school and Tyler's recent illness. But the third time, I was 30, the kids were healthy, we had a stable home and stable jobs. I laughed warmly at her tears but was so confused.

"Mom! Why on Earth are you crying? We wanted to have another baby!" And she said, "I don't know, I just don't want you to be hurt or in pain or stressed. I'm sure it will be fine." They could have been tears of joy, but I think even she wasn't sure.

And I realized, sometimes when the feelings are just too big to express, the best way to get them out is perhaps just a good old boohoo.

Don't judge me.

Miranda Lambert sings about a mother opposite to mine in a song I actually adore, "Mama's Broken Heart." If you haven't heard it, now is the time to look it up on YouTube. (Well not exactly now. Maybe after this chapter would be better.)

Putting on a face for the public has always been an important principle for Southern girls. It's part of our idea of class. Girls that act out are "showing their crazy," we say.

But as I evolve, **I'm finding we can be empowered through our feelings.**

As I consider my journey of growing into a woman, becoming a mother, and facing adversity, I identify one of my greatest challenges as determining my own self-identity, recognizing perhaps who God wants me to be, and battling the desire to conform to a societal standard, all while juggling the complexity of many different roles. Being authentic is difficult if we aren't sure how we feel or who we are, and even when we are sure we have a grasp on that, we often fear how others will view us.

Is nobody who they "post" to be?

Expressing your feelings and being "real" is a common theme on social media these days. But a selfish society, addiction to likes, and the desire for the acceptance of others stops most of us from putting our genuine selves out there.

We all talk about the need to be accepted for who we are, but we are not who we "post" to be. And the need for affirmation is becoming an actual addiction.

CNN published an article in May 2017 regarding research findings from UCLA's brain mapping center. The entire article can be found at https://www.cnn.com/2017/05/19/health/instagram-worst-social-network-app-young-people-mental-health/index.html.

According to lead author Lauren Sherman, "When teens learn that their own pictures have supposedly received a lot of likes, they show significantly greater activation in parts of the brain's reward circuitry. This is the same group of regions responding when we see pictures of a person we love or when we win money."

Furthermore, they shared the results of the study called #Statusofmind. Researchers surveyed almost 1,500 young people aged 14 to 24 on how certain social media platforms impact health and well-being issues such as anxiety, depression, self-identity, and body image. They found that social media platforms demonstrated negative affects overall on young people's mental health.

Not only do we have to worry about kids being criticized or bullied online by others but we also need to worry that kids can be their own worst enemies.

Being presented, or rather barraged, with this large volume of images of others, people who are famous or Insta-famous, the average girl down the street or across the world, everyone from everywhere to compare themselves to, can turn our children's brains into the biggest, meanest critics ever, and put their very beings in the spotlight for evaluation.

"Wow, look at how many likes she has! Maybe more people would like me if I were curvier, or thinner, or if I were blonde, or a redhead. What if I could dance like that or had those clothes?"

As we weather change, it is important to be genuine. For me it was finding my identity as a new mother or figuring out what path I was to take in life or just trying to get through the chaos of life. It is hard not to lose ourselves in the stress and the changes. I found some of my identity and self-worth in "my skin" before I became a mom, but as my body changed, I wasn't even sure if I knew the real me. Part of my identity and strength had been gained from the self-confidence of vanity and attraction, so if that was now distorted, then I wasn't sure what to do to compensate for the loss.

Furthermore, if we spend our time comparing and pretending, we can lose sight of our strengths and weaknesses and drown out the sound of God's voice trying to give us direction.

Only you know the real you.

What if you only became what someone else said you could? What if someone else's opinion of you actually defined who you are? How awful that would be! **They don't know the whole you, the real you!**

Unfortunately, this is a tragedy that happens every single day. Kids are told they are not good enough, not smart enough, not pretty enough. Maybe they don't feel they measure up to what others expect or maybe others don't expect anything so they see no reason to try. They are ashamed that they don't have that many likes or followers.

Who are we when no one is looking? For many, we are not the image we post. We are insecure, too, and hard on ourselves.

Being connected now is not really being connected. Despite the evolving online ecosystem, I am confident there was never a time when other people's opinions didn't matter. They did for me before the social media, before the likes. And I always felt like the way others saw me was limiting. Not the right clothes or hair, what potential could I have? I want to shake that girl in my memories. If social media had been at my fingertips, I would have been doomed to despair. **I didn't know if I could be more, but *I wanted to be more.***

Let good be good and you be you.

Others' opinions have always mattered to us. It's just amplified by social media these days. Don't get me wrong, it is unrealistic to think that anyone will unplug. But when do we stop talking about being real and actually be real? And then when will we be kind enough to *not* criticize or judge anybody else for their authenticity? It is not surprising that anyone would be terrified about any true expressions of self.

Recently, I watched Amy Schumer's standup show, "Leather Special." She talked about her experience in which she posted a revealing picture of herself. Instead of praising her beauty, the media and public called her brave. In her show, she laughed at herself and turned a perceived negative into a positive, but I found this fact that they called her brave to cause me to pause.

I was definitely irritated by this.

Why does society get to set the standard of beauty?

Why do we always have to compare ourselves to others in order to determine how we measure up? Why can't good be good and bad be bad? *Any woman who is strong and healthy and confident is beautiful!* Period. Even the *Bible* calls a virtuous woman more valuable than rubies. On the flip side, we can't whine about not being accepted for being who we are if we are scared to show who we are! **The truth is that others *will* criticize us.** We will be judged.

We would be better off reminding ourselves that the *Bible* teaches us to aim to please God and not man, anyway. *"For am I now seeking the favor of men, or of God? Or am I striving to please men? If I were still trying to please men, I would not be a bond-servant of Christ"* (Galatians 1:10).

One of my favorite quotes of all time though is by Bernard M. Baruch. **"Be who you are and say what you feel, because those who mind don't matter, and those who matter don't mind."**

(Baruch was best known for his role in our government from 1916 to 1948. How interesting that these words spoken so long ago are so timeless!)

Regardless of technology and innovation and how we communicate with each other, every generation still battles degrees of judgment and discrimination. We are divided by our socioeconomic statuses, religions, races, sexual orientations, political views, and even how much you weigh, and so on and so forth . . . **the way in which we judge and compare each other is like a plague we cannot seem to shake.**

Refuse to die!

So, what medication do we have to rid ourselves of this? Like most plagues, you cannot completely rid the population of it unless (you can guess; you've seen the horror movies)...

1) You quarantine it completely and contain it, and 2) Everyone who came into contact with it dies quickly.

Unfortunately, if we continue to pass it on from one person to the next, one generation to the next, it will never go away. So, we have to be stronger than the average victim. We have to be immune to it.

More than ever, it is impossible to keep ourselves safely locked away from negativity, but you can be strong and confident and beautiful and real. You can focus on God's message of love and salvation that makes you whole.

If only...

If only life were like a Coca-Cola commercial, everyone happy and smiling, while singing "I'd Like to Teach the World to Sing (In Perfect Harmony)."

But it's not.

So, what can we do? Well, I'm not always right, and I battle with feeling flawed and comparing myself to others and to past versions of myself, and not just sometimes but every day! So, this is my action plan:

1. When I want to cry, I cry (happy, sad, irrational, it makes no difference). I grrrrrr when I am frustrated. I laugh when I am happy. When I am anxious and worried, I try my durnedest not to suppress it anymore: I acknowledge it and deal with it. Be free to feel what you feel. Even if the feelings are irrational, they are still valid. They are still yours to feel and you can't change them until you acknowledge them.

2. I strive to be humble, but I give myself credit and take credit when I did a good job. This one was hard to learn! Don't belittle your contributions. It's okay to be happy in your successes. They are blessings. They are an example of cultivating the talent God gave you. The confidence and fulfillment that it brings will help pull you

through the moments when you fall or when others try to tear you down.

3.	I remind myself that the parts make the whole (more on this to come), but a clock doesn't work with just one gear. You are made uniquely and magnificently. You have flaws. You have made mistakes, but you have talents and things about you that are special and wonderful. Never focus on one thing and allow only that to define who you are.

4.	Be unashamed. Being a human on this Earth means that you are imperfect. We all are, but we are also made in God's image. I strive to just be the person God intends me to be. I don't pretend to be the perfect mom or perfect wife or perfect anything, but I post makeup-less selfies and pictures where I know I looked chunky that day but my sister looked beautiful or the boys had the cutest smile. And I am open to criticism and when I hurt someone's feelings, I say I'm sorry.

5.	I am thankful to wake up again each day, and I pray each night at bedtime: "Thank you for your blessings, and please help me be a blessing to others." And with every fiber of my being, I really mean it.

What if your gratitude or compliment made them reconsider their dire state of mind? What if seeing the joy you have in Christ brought someone else into the fold? Wouldn't it all be worth it? What if your simplest form of kindness, like a wildfire, could clean out the clutter of negativity crowding out the forest around you? Even if you didn't impact the entire world, if you impact the world you meet, doesn't that in turn make you stronger like that tree in the forest that needs the water and the sun of positivity? God bestows on you the power to start that fire. You have the power to find strength by shedding the layers that cover up your authenticity put on by trying to find acceptance by the masses. And just what if someone saw the real you and was so impressed, so inspired, that not only did they "like" you, they tried to show off the real them? Wouldn't that be refreshing?

Let's be real here, and answer this… Who are you, anyway?

Well, if you are anything like me or most other people I venture to imagine, this might be the absolute most complicated question in the history of mankind and more so, in the history of womankind! Why is that?

Why are we so hard to define? Depending on our mood or situation or relationship, we shift who we are to meet a need, to make us or someone else more comfortable, to fulfill a role because we don't know what else to do. We have a million different reasons for being a million different things.

Sometimes we change as we grow. Sometimes through learning, sometimes through hurt or exposure, even on our journey as we find who we are in Christ, we adapt. We change for the better or we change for the worse but most of us, we change. And even when we aren't changing, we have many layers.

The perfect recipe.

It's the pieces that make you whole.

I am a mom—that's maybe my favorite piece, but I am also a wife, a daughter, a sister, a granddaughter, and a friend. I am a pharmacist and a leader. I like to problem-solve. I'm a writer. I am a crafter and I really love to paint but I am not nearly as talented as my mom or my second child (a.k.a. my "middle little"). I am a music lover but not a great singer. I love to dance. I like reading and learning. I like school. I like to help people. I am a total foodie, which works against me a bit. I love God and country and others, but I also like a glass of Moscato or a cold margarita from time to time.

If I am not careful, I am a procrastinator, or I can be inconsistent. Lord knows I can get moody, and my cooking style is not always that of a grownup. If given the choice of dressing up or wearing pajamas, I would really rather wear PJs. The only bit of makeup I seem to be able to apply with any type of skill is lip gloss and mascara.

I constantly fight the urge to compare myself to others.

I am good, bad, ugly, and beautiful all wrapped up in the same pair of blue jeans (or suit pants depending on the occasion)—and if you think I am starting to sound like Sally Fields in *Cybil*, you would be wrong.

When all of your eggs were in that basket…

If you let one role, one trait, one moment define who you are, what happens when that one thing changes?

Self-perception is scary, y'all. It is like looking at your bank account halfway between paychecks when you know you have been online shopping way too much this month. The truth hurts sometimes.

You are not, I repeat, you are not going to find perfection.

You are going to find a perfectly blended you.

Again, I tell you, "Those who matter don't mind, and those who mind don't matter." The people who love you, love you for you. Your entire blend of you.

You should love you for you.

Show yourself a little grace and congratulate yourself when you do well. Acknowledge your own hard work. Accept praise. Appreciate the person that you are and know that nobody else is just like you—thank goodness we are not all the same! That would be super boring!

Even the mistakes you made or bad things that may have happened to you have made you who you are.

A butterfly might not look anything like a caterpillar but it still started out as a caterpillar. Never underestimate what you are capable of accomplishing. You have what it takes in the pieces of you. Just put them together to work in your favor, and always love the whole you, even if you don't love all the pieces.

Developing grit doesn't just mean living through hard times, it takes being brutally honest with yourself to find your strength and recognize your beauty, and...

Almost nothing is more beautiful than humble authenticity.

Change the Station

A POSITIVE ENVIRONMENT

The Earth is not the center of the universe. We revolve around the sun.

The sun is the source of light and warmth. It pulls us in and is steady and reliable.

When we want to see, we need the light.

In order to heal our pain, we have to remove ourselves from darkness, denial, and the source of the pain.

"May these words of my mouth and this meditation of my heart be pleasing in your sight Lord, my Rock and my Redeemer" (Psalm 19:14).

I don't *think* I'm crazy...

I tell you this with some hesitation as you may begin to question my sanity but I am confident there was this time that *God changed my radio station.*

I know, I know, it sounds a bit ridiculous even as I write it, and I can assure you that I have gone through all the reasons why this is unlikely and still came to this conclusion.

God is really busy and has extremely important matters to tend to so why would he waste his time concerned with me and my choice of audio entertainment while I'm bopping along I-40? Why or how could there be a truly physical intervention by God? God changing my radio station sounds like stories you hear on TV shows about hauntings or something out of a Frank Peretti novel (and by the way, if you haven't read *This Present Darkness* yet, it is definitely thought-provoking).

I tried to remember a time where I felt God had literally done something physically that could not be explained, and while I am confident there were plenty of times, this one seemed quite a bit more "in your face" than the others.

Here's what happened.

I was driving the roughly four-hour stretch between east of Nashville and Memphis for a work trip. My friends and family will tell you I feel like an inadequate human if I'm not multitasking most every minute of my life.

(Sidebar: My husband may tell you this is maddening because I will take "relax" time to check email or work while I am supposed to be watching a movie with him. He says that a) I am not paying attention, and b) I am not relaxing, which is the purpose of the first task. So again, I'm not perfect and am working diligently on being more present but that's for another book, perhaps.)

My multitasking while driving must consist of something non-distracting and that list is pretty short. It is most often composed of listening to an audiobook (on 1.5x to double speed because it keeps my attention and is more efficient), catching up with someone (usually my mom, my sister, or a close friend) on a hands-free call, or meditation. (Meditation in the car can take the form of quiet thought and prayer time to clear my head or as a form of worship belting out the newest Lauren Daigle song while it blasts through the speakers. That's definitely a way to get yourself in a better head space.)

On this day, I was listening to a little honkytonk music (although I don't think people actually ever call it that anymore) and I was car-aoking (definition: the act of car karaoke) through the country song list my sons had put together on Spotify, and although this type of relaxation is sometimes also very needed, I had a thought.

Did I just say that out loud?

I didn't even say it out loud, but when it's God, He knows your heart and mind and you don't have to.

"How can I spend this time wisely? How can I use this time for good, God?"

And I kid you not, *the station changed.*

It didn't just switch playlists from country to the Christian playlist between songs. No, it stopped mid-song! Mid-song, and I looked at the radio as if it was going to give me some clue, maybe I was getting a text or a phone call, maybe my phone was updating, maybe my battery was low. Something logical or rational. But no, none of that.

It stopped mid-song, paused, and changed to a song on the Christian station.

How should I have responded to that?

I don't know what the appropriate reaction is supposed to be when you have a physical Godly intervention. I was shocked, but *I smiled*.

I smiled so big and so hard with tears welled up in the corners of my eyes. The muscles in my face nearly hurt.

How amazing to know that God can be all places at one time and do all things. He cares enough about each of us to be present with us in such a way that he hears our hearts' desires even in the smallest moments. He comes to our side reliably, dependably, every single time.

It makes me know without a doubt that even when I feel alone, even when I wonder why I am not hearing his voice, maybe it's because he knows "I got this." **When I do really need him, I can see that he is there.**

It makes me think about Peter. In the passage, Matthew 14: 22–33 the whole story plays out.

> *Immediately Jesus made the disciples get into the boat and go on ahead of Him to the other side, while He dismissed the crowd. After He had dismissed them, He went up on a mountainside by Himself to pray. Later that night, He was there alone, and the boat was already a considerable distance from land, buffeted by the waves because the wind was against it. Shortly before dawn Jesus went out to them, walking on the lake. When the disciples saw Him walking on the lake, they were terrified. "It's a ghost," they said, and cried out in fear. But Jesus immediately said to them: "Take courage! It is I. Don't be afraid." "Lord, if it's you," Peter replied, "tell me to come to you on the water." "Come," He said. Then Peter got down out of the boat, walked on the water and came toward Jesus. But when he saw the wind, he was afraid and, beginning to sink, cried out, "Lord, save me!" Immediately Jesus reached out His hand and caught him. "You of little faith," He said, "why did you doubt?" And when they climbed into the boat, the wind died down. Then*

those who were in the boat worshiped Him, saying, "Truly you are the Son of God."

Peter was a disciple. He was not only a believer but he had seen Jesus perform many miracles before. The sea was raging on this particular day. He had enough faith to step out but he also had doubts. Yet even though he began to sink, Jesus reached out to him.

Have you ever seen the movie *The Perfect Storm*? (It stars George Clooney and Mark Wahlberg, so enough said—you should totally watch it!) I imagine this day was something like that.

The passengers of the ship were afraid but these guys were no strangers to the sea and travelling by boat. You know a little bit of rocking and rain would not have caused too much upset. So, Jesus walked out onto the water and had Peter come out there, too.

But God, are you SURE?

Now I don't just love this story because it seems like such an out-there, cool kind of thing to happen. After all, Jesus performed lots of miracles that were, well, super-cool.

I love this story partly because I love the ocean and I am so humbled by it.

I think it is such a perfect example of God's vastness and ability. It really puts his power and what kind of God He is into perspective. Nobody can ever see from one side of an ocean to the other. These massive bodies of water encompass 70 percent of our world, and beneath their surface is a whole other world we barely get to be a part of, and it is wondrous and bewildering and beautiful and dangerous.

From the time I knew that I could wish to be something when I grew up until about the seventh grade, I thought I wanted to be a marine biologist.

Which, in retrospect, is painfully ironic because as an adult I am not a very good swimmer and thus have a phobia of drowning.

And although I'm disappointed swimming is a fear I've yet to overcome, this fear makes me appreciate the ocean that much more. It's like this amazing treasure that's out of reach and the freedom that it represents—floating freely, almost like flying—is almost magical. A drop in the ocean is never in the same place for more than a second. That, too, connotes treasure, freedom, and magic.

There is nothing more powerful on this Earth that I can think of than the ocean. We are helpless to tsunamis and hurricanes. We can predict them sometimes with our fancy technology and prepare to evacuate, but nothing will stop the water from going wherever it wants to go.

So, Peter must have felt tiny as he stepped off that boat. And when I imagine the scene, I picture the swells in the waves to be two and three times taller than his height.

I think about how our circumstances can look so big and so scary.

Peter had been in the water before and our mind and everything that is explainable with the laws of this Earth tell us that we cannot stand on the water. It's all about surface tension and buoyancy. With a surfboard we can do it, but nothing logical says to step out with our feet onto the surface of the water. Nothing says, "Do it! You will totally float! Go ahead and walk around out there in those crazy waves!"

This is the second reason I love this story.

Sometimes *Faith* doesn't seem logical.

I am a logical person. I usually take time to analyze a situation before making a decision, though I admit there have been plenty of times I've made impulsive choices or just plain bad ones.

I have taken many leadership tests, and I love any quiz or analysis on self-perspective, because I feel like I can't make myself better if I don't really know me. Since any person's perception is their version of reality, I want my perception to be as close to the actual truth as possible or my efforts will be wasted.

In all of these tests, I come out as the analytical type.

Now, at first this surprised me. I have more instances than I can count where I didn't make the best decision, or made an impulsive decision, and regretted it so much. But once I started to think, and—well, let's say "analyze" myself and my actions, I realized how true the assessment was.

It is one of the reasons that I do so often regret decisions that I make in haste, even if they turn out okay. I turn the bad decisions over and over again in my head, even if I've already thoughtfully weighed them out, because I feel like my analysis was bad or insufficient. I analyze over what I could have done differently.

Recognizing our tendencies for behavior allows us to more effectively use them to our benefit. It also helps us to identify times where the behavior is inhibitive or detrimental, and this, in turn, allows us to recognize and change or avoid the behavior in those circumstances.

As usual, knowledge is power!

But, being analytical can absolutely be contradictive to faith and hope.

When you are analytical and logical and rational, as I am, you need to weigh the good, the bad, and the ugly of the current facts and the possibilities efficiently enough to make a sound decision in a timely manner. Sometimes, that means that you don't weigh the more unlikely possibilities as heavily as the more likely possibilities because your logic finds them to be less realistic and thus less important of a consideration.

When making everyday routine decisions, this method works.

For example, I don't weigh all the pros and cons when deciding to wear heels with an outfit. Pros: Heels will match and look cute and more professional than my favorite sneaks. Cons: Heels are uncomfortable, and if I step into a crack or on a rock, I could fall. If I fall, I could ruin my pants and possibly break my ankle, which would not only be painful: It would also cost me a lot of money in medical bills. Since we are renovating the house, I have no extra money and since I have no extra money to pay for medical bills, then I probably shouldn't wear these heels. I'm not going to wear them.

No! That sounds really extra, doesn't it?

I just say, these are cute and can I tolerate wearing them all day? Yes, okay, great! I'm wearing them!

But when making more long-term impactful decisions like a career change or moving or marriage or whatever, thorough analysis can be super helpful.

So…how does this play into planning for what God can do?

This one, no doubt, is a tough question. I have seen God pull some amazing stuff out of that hat. He has intervened in ways that I would not, could not ever possibly dream up as possible, much less likely, scenarios.

So, are we supposed to have blind faith or are we supposed to make "smart" choices? **Is it irrational to believe in a miracle?**

I am so glad you asked! While I cannot claim to be the expert (I do not have a degree in theology) I can tell you my approach and, drawing from my experience, what I think.

I analyze, I assess what I can do.

I believe that God gave me abilities, talents, and experiences to help me help myself *and* to help others, **and that's what I plan for.**

I *pray.* I seek advice from those who are strong in faith. I read God's word. The *Bible* says that wisdom comes from the Lord, so I seek it. I plan and know that I must be patient to understand that I can show up. I can do the best that I can. Things still won't always go the way that I planned or intended, and that's where the faith comes in. I stay open to guidance in His will and understanding that there is purpose in the circumstances, even if they cause us pain.

I try to make smart choices.

I try to do what I think is best for me and others, and I pray for guidance to act as God would intend for me to. *"Trust in the LORD with all thine heart; and lean not unto thine own understanding. In all thy ways acknowledge Him, and He shall direct thy paths"* (Proverbs 3:5–6).

And then I remind myself:

"I know the plans I have for you, declares the Lord, plans to prosper and not to harm, plans to give you hope and a future" (Jeremiah 29:11).

God is bigger than the waves.

I am not going to lie to you. If I were Peter, I know I would have been scared and overwhelmed, especially since I am a horrible swimmer. When Peter started to look around at the ocean and waves and the thought of how irrational it was for him to be able to stand above that water, all of it seemed so illogical.

He started to sink.

How many times have you looked at your circumstances and felt yourself starting to sink?

Peter became afraid and cried out to Jesus. There is a hymn that was sung at my small family church when I was growing up, and whenever I think of it, I only hear it in my head in my Aunt Trisha's voice:

"Greater is He that is in me. Greater is He that is in me. Greater is He that is in me, than he that is in the world."

When I was young, I knew it was about God, but honestly, I really had no idea other than it sounded like the tongue twister challenges we liked to play. But today I know. I know that we are just like Peter.

Despite the circumstances, despite the waves and the laws of physics, all Peter had to do was focus on Jesus and what He wanted him to do, and Peter could rise above the ocean beneath. He would not be swallowed up by circumstance.

When you have sought his wisdom and direction and planned using that and all the facts you have, when you have done everything that you can do that makes sense, and it still seems like it isn't working out, all that is required is focus on God. **That is when our faith and His provision can supersede the logical.**

He is not a genie in a bottle. He is not here to grant a wish. Quite the opposite!

We are here as vessels and if you believe the scripture, that His plans for those that love Him are to succeed and prosper, then yes, it may feel like He is working magic for you. But while you are in control of your actions and reactions, you are not in control of God. However, living in His will, taking actions in line with that, is like a divine collaboration, and we all know how much more we can do when we work as a team, right?

Stop looking at the waves.

Change *your* station.

If your focus seems to stray, if you feel your feet start to sink, maybe it is time for you to look away from your waves and to change your station.

Let the music of faith, of positivity, of joy, of worship and gratitude come in through your ears, vibrate from your eardrums to your most fundamental molecules, and let it change your mood, your state of mind, your direction. Let it change your heart and resonate in your soul.

Will it really make a difference?

You might not know this but music plays a part in medicine!

Dr. Freda Lewis Hall, the Chief Patient Officer at Pfizer, has been featured on the television show *The Doctors* at least twice discussing the benefits and importance of music therapy in patients with some medical conditions such as epilepsy and other disorders. These disorders have something in common, they originate in the brain.

Music therapy is a subset of pediatric patient care at Vanderbilt Children's Hospital in Nashville. The music therapists are board certified and are involved in creating individualized treatment plans for the kids. They use music interventions to help with chronic pain, psychiatric symptoms, procedural support, general coping, and in end of life therapy, just to name a few. The family is also involved when possible to optimize outcomes.

On a recent episode, a teen patient at Vanderbilt, Donal, was featured. He had uncontrolled seizures with the use of medicine alone. After Donal had invasive testing to map the brain activity, his therapists used a music project. They created and performed a song in his favorite style, rap, to get through some of the complex feelings he was having. The music provided him an outlet to express his feelings in a positive way and helped him to cope with what was happening as he prepared for his next procedure. It gave Donal something to be excited about and a way for his family and healthcare providers to connect with him. Ultimately, it made for an environment that was conducive for communication and healing.

And pediatrics is just the beginning! Studies with music are also being done in other areas, such as brain trauma and dementia, to help patients regain memory function.

What else can music do?

There is also a study that reported that plants exposed to music had a different growth outcome depending on the sounds played in their environment.

I like to think of myself as a scientist first. But of all people, my mother, the artist, told me about this study. I basically wrote it off as ludicrous! My mother is very much a "speak life" cheerleader, so of course she would believe this, but lo and behold, when I searched for studies regarding plants and the effect of music, I hit on a variety of sources for information on this.

One article published in the *International Journal of Environmental Science and Development* (Vol. 5, No. 5, October 2014), details the effect of different types of music on Rosa Chinensis plants. In this study, Vidya Chivukula and Shivaraman Ramaswamy detail the assessment of 30 plants. They were divided into five groups, each of which was subjected to one of the following music types: Indian classical music, Vedic chants, Western classical music, and rock music, and one group as the control was kept in silence.

The researchers assessed elongation of plant shoot, internode elongation, number of flowers, and diameter of flowers. It was speculated that while frequency and vibration were factors that affected the results, the plants exposed to Vedic chants and classical music definitively had more robust growth.

With my always analytical and skeptical hat on, I thought about all of the possible contributing variables that may have been part of studies such as these.

The plants were all grafted on the same day from a single mother plant, potted in uniform soil, and in similarly sized pots, but maybe, inadvertently, some plants had better care than others. Were light, and amount of food, and measure of nutrients absolutely exact? If not, could minute differences have had an impact? What about air moisture and pressure?

But I also thought about how not just music but positive "vibes," in general, *do* affect me.

I thought that speaking negatively could not bring doom to pass, and I still can't say for sure whether that's true or not, but I can say that every morning on the way to the hospital, my husband and I and Tyler listened to Third Day, a Christian rock band, and their music calmed me.

Despite how I was raised, I rarely listened to Christian music outside of church. I listened to anything from Vivaldi to AC/DC to Nelly. Those were among my favorites back then, but not really Christian music. I liked for my music to reflect my mood, and although I had been redeemed by the grace of God, my personal relationship with him wasn't strong. I didn't recognize it to be a top priority for him or myself. I didn't understand the need to cultivate it like you would a friendship or your relationship with your spouse. And, I didn't desire that closeness to God that I do now.

And even while, from minute to minute during those rocky times, my faith went from strong to wavering and my mood from angry to scared, *hearing* songs of praise and worship that spoke of grace and goodness and a kind and faithful God began to speak to my soul and *give me peace*.

This realization broke my walls but built my foundation.

I may have still felt blind to the future, but I felt I had a hand to hold and guide me through the darkness.

It gave me a confidence that we could deal with whatever was next and that there would be a light at the end.

So, while I can't say from a scientific perspective that what you hear will change your circumstances, maybe it can change you, your state of mind. **Maybe it can calm your inner storm and give you an environment conducive to healing.**

Maybe you need to change the station.

This Ain't No Sob Story

AND NEITHER IS YOURS

Is it true that my family has met its fair share of challenges? Yes.

Is it always easy and uneventful to have a child with a disability? No.

Are there days where I still feel scared, inadequate, or defeated? Yes.

"We are afflicted in every way, but not crushed; perplexed but not driven to despair; persecuted but not forsaken; struck down, but not destroyed" (2 Corinthians 4:8–9).

But let me tell you that this story, my story, our story—in case you can't tell by now—ain't no sob story!

And guess what, yours ain't either!

I hope at this point you are on the same page as me, but in case you may still be asking yourself why I feel like I am entitled to give any advice on overcoming adversity or building resilience, or in case you may be wondering what my perfect life looks like now, I will share a little more.

Life is being full-time working parents with three active boys: Two teenagers and a seven-year-old. Life is raising a child with a disability. Life is dedicating myself to leadership and volunteering and Christ.

I am not going to mince words. It is *work*. It is tiresome and challenging, and I don't always know that I am prioritizing appropriately or that I am making the best decisions.

I still need help, encouragement, validation, and guidance.

Learning to lean.

As confident and strong as I may feel professionally when I have had a kickass day at work, I may still come in and see the laundry pile and dishes. I know we have wrestling scheduled that night, and I know I need help!

Billy is my partner. Billy helps me.

Are we the perfect couple? No.

Have we always had a collaborative, amazing relationship? Gosh no!

So, if you have a partner and you are undergoing something so scary and so stressful it is putting strain on your relationship, then maybe you can find value in this:

We were a couple for three years before our first child came. We were basically kids ourselves, of course, and we acted as such. Our relationship had highs and lows that would rival the best attractions at Six Flags. We had fun together, we laughed together, we could each be so incredibly thoughtful, we had passionate, exciting, intoxicating sex, and when we fought, we cut to the core with our words and actions. We were jealous and spiteful and petty.

When Tyler was born, we had to grow up a little. When he got sick, we had to grow up a lot, and when you go through something that breaks you down, and you go through it with a partner, the way you treat each other will either build you back stronger than you were before or it will completely destroy you down to the foundation.

I have seen this happen. **If you are not on the same page in how to deal with the circumstances, you are very much at risk for the latter.**

We didn't make a pact or have a profound conversation on how we would move forward. I think it was more the nonverbal communication that got us through. We tried to tune in to what the other person needed and pick up on the cues. We did everything we could as partners. We felt like nobody else on Earth could possibly understand our situation—our grief, loss of normal life, our fear.

Billy really became my best friend.

We grew together, not apart, and that set the precedent for our relationship moving forward. We would lean on each other. We didn't even have to share our feelings—just a look or a hug was enough. We tried to keep Tyler happy and get him healthy and help him feel like he was both normal and special at the same time, if that were even possible.

I think knowing what the other person needs as well as trying to recognize what you need, and communicating that, are really what is key.

Appreciate the differences.

I need Billy's realism to ground me, and he needs my optimism to have faith. He likes the role as the protector and the strong one, and I assume my place as a Southern belle. After all, I grew up watching how strong Scarlett O'Hara was, even though everyone underestimated her (it was, and still is, my mom's favorite movie of all time). And when we parent, Billy tells the boys where they can improve, and I just dote on them.

And he's not wrong, but neither am I. **Every good team needs a coach and cheerleaders!** And while the importance of the cheerleader may be minimized, I believe it gives the encouragement and positivity and energy needed to carry out the coach's advice. He's the yin to my yang.

Putting the "ABLE" in disable.

This brings me to the question of raising a well-rounded, confident young man who also has a disability. There is a delicate balance that lies in encouraging and pushing. I definitely don't take all the credit.

When I said this isn't a sob story, I meant it.

It's much more than that: it's a success story!

Tyler has become a compassionate young man with a warm, dimpled smile, and he still has the fighter spirit.

He loves and seeks God. He has friends and a girlfriend. He drives and makes good grades. He is independent and driven. He himself has become a mentor.

Finding community through organizations like the Challenged Athletes Foundation and the Amputee Coalition of America not only gave him friends he would bond to for life but that he could truly relate to. It also gave him exposure to extraordinary people whom he could look up to. They have challenges just like his own and knowing them allows him to set the highest goals. It also allows him to see that reaching these goals is possible if he works hard and believes in himself.

"But they that wait upon the Lord shall renew their strength; they shall mount up

with wings as eagles, they shall run and not grow weary, and they shall walk and not faint" (Isaiah 40:31).

This was the *Bible* verse we chose for Tyler's dedication at Southaven First Baptist, shortly after we found out he was sick. **It was hard to believe fervently that this would be his future, one of strength and speed, back then.** It was hard to believe that Tyler could ever "run like a guinea" as the old missionary had prophesied.

Although running was a real challenge for many years (my heart broke when he said he loved to race at recess; it wasn't fair because he couldn't seem to win), he never lost his love of racing.

When we found out about adaptive sports, that put him in a new playing field. And after that, there really was no turning back. He made the internationally competitive USA adaptive track team and competed in Ireland this past year in many events. The 100-meter and 200-meter dashes are his favorites.

Currently, he is striving to make the Paralympic team. He has a very real chance, thanks to the Challenged Athletes Foundation. They give him—and us!—support and resources, and his coaches and team at the North Jersey Navigators have become family to us. His doctors and prosthetists ensure he is in tip-top shape.

He went to Thailand with Clemson University to help teach adaptive sports at a college in Chang Mai. He loves travelling, serving, and making new friends, so you can imagine how amazing this experience was for him.

His freshman year, he decided he wanted to wrestle on his high school team. And although I was nervous, watching him wrestle under the spotlight without his leg on was one of my proudest moments as his mom. In the middle of that mat, his disability felt more pronounced as he and his opponent squared off, the opponent looking down on him from their two firm feet planted, as

Tyler took a knee. He seemed so exposed, in front of his opponent and in front of this crowd of spectators.

Yet his eyes were focused on his opponent's face. Tyler's strong physique was evident in his singlet, and when the buzzer sounded, he was quick and strong. He reminded me of an octopus when he caught his opponent in his grip, unrelenting. That season he went on to win second place in Tennessee for Junior Varsity.

It was that experience that drove home for me something so important that I'd been learning all along but just never clicked.

Success is not defined by where you are but by how far you've come.

Every wrestling tournament, Tyler started from his knee. Without his right leg, the struggle would always be harder for him in some ways than his opponent. So even when he lost, there was something to be proud of. But winning truly was defined as conquering adversity.

Tyler has *grit*.

He had watched many YouTube videos of Anthony Robles, amputee and former NCAA champ, and was lucky enough to meet him once at a CAF event. Tyler believed if Anthony could win against these "able-bodied" guys, then he could, too.

Anthony was a beast on the mat. Tyler studied his techniques and how he strategized to overcome the disadvantage of having the one leg, and he believed in himself. He trained hard. He won most improved wrestler on his team that first year. His competition was always lean, strong, and often fierce and experienced. But Tyler would leave it all out there on the mat.

He didn't place varsity every match, and he didn't always win, but he always gives it 200 percent. There have been times when he has heard a comment from the other team that was diminishing of his abilities. "Don't worry, you go up against that kid with one leg next. It should be easy." While hurtful, these comments would fuel Tyler and more often than not, he would win those matches.

Tyler's disability was just as much his opponent on the mat as was the other kid.

I realized that it's not fair to compare ourselves to others because we don't know where they started.

We have to take our adversity to the mat, and we have to give ourselves credit and recognize that even if we didn't beat the other guy, we started from a knee.

Scarred but not broken.

Tyler wants to dedicate his life to a career helping others find healing and strength. This is another blessing that has emerged from "our curse."

He is in so many ways my hero.

What I found when winging it.

Love comes first. **Love fiercely**.

You cannot protect your children from everything, but you can teach them.

Prepare them for the fact not all people are nice. Teach them that those people must not affect you. Not all things are easy, but if they are something you want, then it's worth working for. Remind them to not feel sorry for themselves.

No matter how challenged you are, you can become stronger.

No matter how sad you are, there is somebody else whose mountains to climb are higher and steeper.

You are capable, you are special for many reasons, and your disability whatever it may be **doesn't define who you are**. But accomplishing your biggest goals in spite of it does make you stronger than the average bear.

You are a person like everybody else. You are not perfect and you will make mistakes, but also try to do what you believe in your heart is right.

If it doesn't work out, make sure your kids know you will always be there for them.

And most importantly, pray, believe God's promises, trust him, and know that He intends all things for the good of those who love Him.

I strive to instill these values in my other two kids as well. In the amputee community, moms refer to them as "all-bits kids" because they are not missing any limbs. This may lead you to ask, how do you give your child with a disability the proper amount of attention without overlooking your all-bits kids?

After all, you haven't heard much about my other kids up to this point, even.

Again, I will be frank with you, it is a challenge, and I don't just speak from my own personal experience. This is something many of my friends who have kids with similar challenges say they can totally relate to.

Finding ways to allow physically challenged children to participate on an equal playing field and opportunities that allow them to connect and bond with others that are "like them" means travel, money, and time.

How do you prevent this from becoming a vacuum that leaves your other kids feeling very unfairly neglected? How do you keep them from feeling like offspring born to be a cheering section for the child that is "special?"

To put it quite simply, it must be intentional. And every few months, Billy and I have to sit down and have a frank conversation about whether or not Tyler is getting all the attention.

It is so important that you recognize the interests and talents of your other children and then ensure that they get time to be in the spotlight and time to be connected to you. In other words, put their stuff on the calendar in Sharpie, not pencil.

Peyton is my middle son. He and I went to California last year to see San Francisco, Monterey Bay, and Yosemite with a group from his school. He loves science and solving problems, and I love his endless curiosity. We made memories I will always cherish. One of my favorites was crossing the Bay Bridge together. I felt so small and also so blessed to be taking in the beauty, the experience, and the special moment with my son.

Easton is my youngest. I try to eat lunch with him at the elementary school at least once per week. He gets giddy about us being able to sit in the tables outside the main cafeteria—they're meant just for the kids whose parent can visit. Sometimes his friend sits with us, too, but even when he doesn't, Easton still gets excited for me to join him and this makes me feel so special! He also still likes to cuddle with me on the couch when we watch movies.

I soak in every moment with each of them.

I have spent little time in this book telling you about the everyday challenges of motherhood, career, or marriage and I have barely mentioned my other two children whom I love dearly, but it's not because that part of my life is less important. **We have learned from the adversity to be grateful for the moments in our life that are blissful and beautiful and, quite honestly, boring!** It is the biggest blessing to realize when you are living in moments of peace. I don't want you to read this book and walk away with simple tips and tricks about navigating normal daily life. I want you to be strong enough to conquer "the big stuff."

Once you can do that, it puts everything else into perspective. You can relish in the normal. I still have plenty of daily struggles! But I have found contentment amidst the chaos and conflict, and that's what I clung to once the dust settled.

MY HEART IS FULL.

Peyton:

Peyton is incredibly artistic, like my mom. He is good at wrestling and was a fabulous little baseball player like his dad was. He is intellectual and likes science and documentaries like me. He is witty and funny, and although I'm not entirely sure where that comes from, I love it. As middle children are often reported to prefer time alone to time with others, he is also quite content—well, let's be honest, quite *intent*—to have his fair share of "me time." He likes video games that involve strategy. He is my child who will spend twice the time it would take to complete a task trying to figure out a more efficient way to accomplish it.

He truly seems to care little about others' opinions of him but has such a tender heart when receiving critical feedback—his pride is likely one of his biggest hurdles, and he really, really hates to lose at anything. He is the one who will help me in the kitchen and would be the one most likely to sign up for a survival show. Right now, he wants to grow up to be a plastic surgeon, a way to combine art and medicine and science. **I love him completely and uniquely.**

Easton:

Easton is very much the littlest brother. He plays the role so well. He has a nose and chin like Tyler but Peyton's adorable freckles and startling blue eyes. Easton smiles with his whole entire face; his smile turns his eyes into little slits to see from. You cannot look at Easton happy and giddy and not smile with him. He never ever wants to do anything by himself, not even sleeping.

He knows that with four bigger people in the family, there is usually a pretty good chance that, with a little begging, somebody will play with him or get him whatever he needs or snuggle with him while he plays a game or watches a movie.

He gets his wit from Peyton and likes to be surrounded by friends and activity like Tyler. He also loves to draw and read and learn new things. He is a whiz at technology, can hit a golf ball like a miniature pro, and nothing makes him happier than a little positive praise. He said he wants to live next door to me when he grows up, and he also wants to be a doctor. (Because why not if his brothers are?) **I also love him completely and uniquely.**

I am who I am because of these people.

I might have contributed to the creation of three of these amazing humans but they have also helped me to grow. I couldn't have earned my MBA without Tyler and Peyton pitching in to help with their baby brother. We couldn't do all the things that we have to do—travel for work, soccer, wrestling, Cub Scouts, track, wheelchair basketball, make dinner, do laundry—if every member of this family didn't pitch in and play a part. Billy helped me figure out not only who I am but who I wanted to become and he supports me in everything so that I can get there.

If you expect life to be smooth sailing just because you get through what feels like the worst of the worst you have ever experienced, I am sorry to say it might not be.

Actually, it probably won't be, but the courage and resilience and wisdom you gain through the storm will make everything else feel more like foothills than mountains to climb.

So, no, my story is not a sob story, and neither is yours.

You might be in a really scary, rocky time, but every story worth reading has conflict and villains and heroism and love. If you haven't slayed your dragon yet or met your prince, that just means that **better chapters are to come.**

Endless Flaws

SUCCESS IS NOT DETERMINED BY MEASURE OF PERFECTION

Just because I sparkle, doesn't mean I'm shiny.

I am not smooth and polished. I am complex, and my life has been kind of messy. I haven't always been sure of my path or purpose, and I definitely didn't always end up on the road most travelled.

But glitter goes on in layers, not in a row, and I'm happy with that.

Perfection on its own doesn't guarantee success or strength or resilience. We have all fallen short, and true perfection in our world does not exist. Striving for perfection in areas of your life may contribute to success, but a lot of other great characteristics can get you there.

The best people, like the best desserts, are layered.

So, if you are wondering if all the mistakes you've made, or where you come from, or who you are today means that you cannot and will not ever overcome, you will be happy to learn tomorrow is a new day. Your next action can be independent of your last.

God offers us an opportunity to be redeemed, to be made new and forgiven by His grace.

"Therefore, if anyone is in Christ, he is a new creation. The old has passed away; behold, the new has come" (2 Corinthians 5:17).

What are you hiding under there?

In June of 1997, I became a promiscuous teen.

I can list a million reasons why I don't want to talk about this. At the inception of this book, I had no intention of telling it.

I have hidden that part of me, that dark secret, and have built a life around it, like you would bury a time capsule in the ground and build a house on top of it, hoping that by the time anybody ever opened it, I would be dead a million years.

Every accomplishment and sparkling happy moment is another brick in the wall that would ensure that nobody in my life as an adult would see the dirt that I could not wash away.

So why?

Why would I share this now? Why would I divulge what I consider to be the ugliest part of me to a world that mostly doesn't see it and if they did, they don't talk about it?

Why would I allow those I love who may not know this shameful thing about me to now hear it?

I won't share the number here because I think whether it is higher or lower than your number makes no difference. The point is how my number, my actions, made me feel about myself. It is our habitual comparison of ourselves to others that we use to define ourselves that leads to the demise of our feeling of self-worth. Worse, it is our basis to judge others.

I tell you this because I want you to recognize that you can learn from your mistakes. You can admit you were wrong, and you can repent. **Even the shiniest of smiles has been polished with flaws and regret and mistakes. Yet the Lord of all creation still loves you. You can forgive yourself, too.** You can still love yourself and believe in yourself and take good from every hard situation.

My mother will be ashamed to read, and my husband may be embarrassed or sad that I feel the need to relay this (although he knows my every worst moment and still loves me), and I have *never* wanted my kids to hear that there was this side of me that I am not proud of, but I need all of them to know what I believe is true: You can be a good person even if you have done things you are not proud of. The saying "nobody is perfect" is not meant to be an excuse about our own lousy behavior but simply a reminder to forgive ourselves and others as God forgives us, if we ask.

There is redemption in recognition.

Here is the dirt. I was for the most part a happy kid, I think. We weren't rich, but I always lived in a clean house, my clothes always fit, and we always had cable.

However, I do also remember living in a single-parent home. My clothing was hand-me-downs or from a thrift store. Oftentimes, my mom made my clothes and I was always a little petrified that someone in my class would recognize my "newest" sweater.

I was shy, actually, which will be a surprise to most who know me now and I think awkward. I was nervous about trying new things. It took me until second grade to ride my bike without training wheels.

I had horribly untamable hair. It was long and not straight but not curly either. It was more like confused, or rebellious. My mom always brushed it for me in the morning, but it was always tangled and ridiculous in no time. Also, I couldn't wear it in a ponytail because of that thing where I felt like my ears were big, and the first time another kid pointed them out—well then, I was stuck with the crazy hair. I also didn't like sandals or wear flip-flops until college because I thought my toes were too long.

Please do not make the mistake of feeling sorry for me.

I am not trying to make myself out to be a victim. I was not hurt or abandoned or abused.

I want you to see how perspective is everything!

Wearing the cloak of negativity.

Why are we our own worst enemy? Why are we so adept at finding the bad in everything, including ourselves, especially ourselves, and focusing on it? Why do we become discontent when we aren't in tune to God's purpose for our life?

"Do not love this world nor the things it offers you, for when you love the world, you do not have the love of the Father in you. For the world offers only a craving for physical pleasure, a craving for everything we see, and pride in our achievements and possessions. These are not from the Father, but are from this world.

And this world is fading away, along with everything that people crave. But anyone who does what pleases God will live forever" (1 John 2:15–17).

I had lots of good things in my life—love. My parents loved me. My grandparents loved me. My family was close. I spent almost every day with my great Aunt Cille who made literally the best chocolate pie I have ever had in my life. Aunt Cille taught me how to needlepoint when I was five (not a skill I still use, but I have good memories nonetheless). My Uncle Bob made his own wine, and since my mom didn't allow alcohol of any kind in our house I found this to be super intriguing and very cool!

Every afternoon, I was at my grandma's with my cousins. I was the oldest by a little and there were usually about five of us at least, including my sister. I loved being the leader and helping "care" for the little ones, especially my little sister. There wasn't much to do so we made our own adventures. I am sure we didn't realize how lucky we had it. My Grandma Vevian is the strongest and most faithful woman I've ever known. She made big, elaborate, home-cooked Southern meals every day and we all ate there and helped clean up. We snapped peas from the garden and shucked corn. I miss that.

I didn't have a lot of friends outside of my cousins, but I wanted to be just like the friends I did have. I can still remember my first sleepover with my best friend in kindergarten. We went to the amusement park that day, and I thought her family was the coolest. Her dad was funny and her mom was lovely and precious, and my friend Laura, had the cutest high-top sneakers with different color ribbons for shoestrings and the coolest hair bows.

Even a few years later, when her parents got divorced, I only saw the fun stuff. Her new stepdad bought her a new 4-wheeler and we spent hours riding around. At her dad's house, we always got pizza and had the best time.

So, when my dad and mom got a divorce, why was it not cool? I grew up in a very religious home and nobody in my family was divorced that I can recall. I realize now that even though I was in the fourth grade, the first time my dad left a note and didn't come home, he unknowingly impacted my self-perception for years.

In my dad's eyes, he wasn't leaving us, he was leaving *her*. My mom was in shock, and I had never seen them fight, so I was so confused. I am still quite unsure about all the things that happened in my house that I never saw, but I remember being so puzzled.

What could be more important than us?

I didn't really know what sex was exactly, as I was not even allowed to watch anything rated more severe than PG, but I overheard my mom and her friend talking about how they couldn't believe my dad would leave his family for sex with "that woman." They said this in a Loretta Lynn drawl to emphasize their distaste and anger.

I wondered what was so bewitching about sex that you would actually just leave your family? It seemed like a fantasy, or a movie, in which my dad must have swept this lady up in some elaborate romantic way. Then they'd go off into a sunset with no kids and no responsibilities. Later I learned, of course, it wasn't that extravagant at all.

I remember when he came home to get his clothes and wanted to hug me goodbye despite my dramatics. I made a scene, running onto the front yard, crying, plopping onto the front stoop. He just kissed the back of my head and pulled away anyway. To me it was clear: I wasn't a priority. They reconciled once or twice but it always ended the same, and by the time I was in seventh or eighth grade, they were done for good, I think.

Get ahold of yourself!

I thought she was weak and naive. I had been enamored by my dad. I wanted him to take me fishing (I was not really a fishing kind of girl but it was something I knew he would like) and I wanted to play with my Barbies in the garage while he worked on old cars. After that day on the stoop, I was bitter.

My mom cried and cried and cried. Not like a boohoo cry but like she was losing her sanity and her-guts-were-twisting-in-two kind of wailing. Watching my mom change before my eyes into this broken being didn't make me just sorry for her but it made me think, **"That will *never* be me."**

Love and divorce became like a sad country song, and I saw myself Miranda Lambert-ing past the pain. I was angry.

Invisible...

Regardless of how old you are, not knowing your worth, feeling irrelevant, and not having any sense of a purpose can be disorienting. By high school, things at home were hard. I made good grades but didn't have many friends. Your socioeconomic status by high school was tied to the brands you wear, and how do you explain that to your single mom when the bank just fore-closed on your house? You don't.

The friends I did have were changing. Their priorities were changing and social circles were shifting. I had changed. **I felt invisible.** I wasn't important to anyone it seemed. My mom was distracted with moving on. I didn't know what my life had in store for me but so far I saw nothing interesting.

If you define yourself by what others think of you, well, what if they think nothing at all? When you set your goals by what you see, what if you see nothing in your future?

I became the villain in my own story!

I met "him" at church. I wasn't really allowed to go anywhere else. He was older than me and had a girlfriend, I think, and afterwards (after we "did it") he said he liked me but he really just wanted to know what it was like to be with a virgin. Then he kind of thanked me for that.

This makes me feel pitiful and pathetic and sad for the girl I was back then, when I think about her. But he was a teenager, too. He didn't love me, I didn't love him. I wasn't confused by that. I wasn't forced or assaulted. It was my choice.

I wanted to feel seen, and wanted, and in control.

Everything about my upbringing taught me right from wrong. I was raised to not just go to church every Sunday morning, every Sunday evening, and Wednesday night, but that God has a personal relationship with all who let him. But I had even seen my dad stand behind the pulpit and preach before and I had seen my mom trust God wholly and **look at us now**, I thought.

Also, I was shy and depressed and angry, and I wanted to be something else, anything else, and maybe this would change me. Maybe sex would make me powerful and interesting. I wanted to feel something like love, and *maybe* this was the closest I could get.

It wouldn't be the last time it happened, and it didn't get me what I wanted.

After that my shorts got shorter, my shirts got tighter, and for the next few months, there were a couple of guy friends that got to have sex with me more than a couple of times.

I was never a huge risk-taker, and I was always smart enough to use protection. Even though I knew the ball was in my court, for a while back then I still resented them for taking advantage of my inability to say no. Maybe it wasn't an inability. Maybe it was more apathy, or rebellion, or maybe all of it combined.

I was desperate for the attention, or maybe connection. Honestly for me, it was more about what it was like for them to like me and not even so much about me liking them. It was about the positive feedback and maybe a sense of power.

It wasn't their fault. **They were just playing a part in my own actions of destruction**.

I drank alcohol, too, and smoked cigarettes for a brief time. **I wanted to numb all the cuts from the sharp edges I couldn't seem to smooth.** I felt like other girls thought I wasn't as good as they were. I couldn't control that, but I could be something else. These guys didn't want to marry me or even be my boyfriend, and I didn't want that either. But when it was over, I had nothing again.

"And the Lord will guide you continually and satisfy your desire in scorched places and make your bones strong; and you shall be like a watered garden, like a spring of water, whose waters do not fail" (Isaiah 58:11).

I was looking in the wrong places for fulfillment.

How could this end well?

That one summer was like that movie *13*, where you don't know whether to feel sorry for the main character or disgusted or angry. But you know that since you can't intervene from the other side of the television, this is not going to end well. And, you aren't really sure who to blame exactly.

If I were a girl today, it probably would have manifested into a permanent record of bad behavior as a picture on a cell phone. I'd be dying inside, just for the sake of a million likes.

My heart aches for today's teens. I am thankful my hard times were not lived online or in permanent pixels.

Then August came, junior year. I made the decision to dry my tears, cross my legs, put my head down, and just get through the rest of high school without killing myself or ruining my life.

I wasn't in a better place. **I just realized my actions hadn't made me happier, gotten me anywhere, or earned me anything** (respect, envy, love, anything) except maybe some whispers behind my back, "Did you hear what she did?" Why should they (these boys) get any enjoyment from me when I was not feeling any better myself? Anyway, it wasn't that fun anymore.

A new day, A new beginning.

It was roughly 60 days after that I met Billy. Full disclosure, I don't want my boys to propose to anybody at 16 years old or even anytime soon after that. This is not going to get all *Coal Miner's Daughter,* but yes, it got real, and real fast. Billy was from my small town. He was three years my senior, and we met at the football game I told you about earlier.

I am sure he remembers that night differently than me, but I remember his pretty blue eyes, white teeth, and adorable dimples. He had this smile that reeled me in. I had heard about him, this cute guy with the white Mustang, and he was now getting introduced to me by my bestie's boyfriend.

I remembered our exchange across the parking lot. He looked interested as he held my glare, and when we left he gave me a hug and asked for my number.

Within days, I became his everything. **It wasn't perfect**. We were young. Sometimes he was jealous and we could be verbally abusive to each other. We didn't know what we were doing with our life yet, but in three months, I had a diamond on my 16-year-old ring finger.

He was crazy about me. He wanted to see me every day. He told me I was smart and pretty. He believed in me and made me feel special and in a lot of ways protected me. I still had sex but only with him.

I don't condone this now and I'm not proud of my decisions back then, but I am thankful for those memories with him. Sin is still sin, big or small. I recognize it's difficult to follow God's path when our eyes are clouded by transgression, and I have repented for my mistakes. Still it was the most passionate, best sex of our lives. We were free and confident and had no responsibility. He was my prom date, he took me to project graduation, he picked me up from cheer practice, and he bought me my first cell phone (mainly because he hated to have to ask my mom to talk to me when he called my house, but that's beside the point).

He wanted me to lean on him. He saw I needed it when I didn't know that I did. Aside from my longing for independence and my inability to trust fully as motivating factors for my drive for success, his encouragement and support and faith in me are what gave me the courage to believe in myself.

He is still crazy about me, and he still wants to see me every day. We use Facetime when I travel for work. He's still my favorite human and I am his. Even when I have been moody, mean, fat, skinny, weak, or strong, he is always loyal, and he is always there for me.

I don't think God was proud of my actions or my sin, but **I believe he intended to bring good out of the bad.** He knew what I needed when I needed it. And, I believe he **forgave** me.

Not through my history of good actions or because I worked to earn it but because I was remorseful and humble and broken.

Forgiving myself, now that was much harder, and it took years. Forgiving others wasn't easy for me either. Being hard on myself, after that bout of bad judgement, I hold both myself and others to a very high standard. It wasn't fair. I was very judgmental of weakness. I didn't understand my parents' choices. I couldn't see through their lenses. I was hard on my mom because I expected her to be stronger. I was angry at my dad because I felt he was selfish.

It did take years, and now I realize that you can't go back and redo. We can only control our own actions and reactions, and **I don't want to live life bitter**. I forgave them in my heart.

My mom and I are actually very close now, and my dad and I are trying, too, as you've read. I know that the good that came out of it for me is that I am stronger, and I appreciate my husband more even when we are stressed and not getting along.

I eventually forgave me in my heart, too.

Irrational feelings lead to irrational thoughts.

Now, what if I told you that "my number" could be counted on one hand, that I practiced safe sex, and that all of these boys were relatively well known to me and not strangers. Would it change your view of my story?

Well, those are the facts. So, if some of you are pausing to say, "Well, in that case, what you did wasn't *that* big of a deal" and others may be saying "Still, how unacceptable," your response or reaction centers on your personal experiences and perception.

Similarly, for me, my response to my actions was centered around my experience and my perception!

It's why we as a society have a basis for ethical or moral behavior. But depending on the person you ask, there is more gray than black and white.

I can condemn myself much more harshly than anyone else.

I can condemn myself even for bad thoughts or bad intentions that I never set into actions just because I know they were there! **Y'all, nobody is perfect,** so I *still* struggle with this expectation that I set for myself based on the way that I was raised. When I am in control of my actions, sin is sin, no matter how big or small. It can overshadow all the good in the world, I have seen it happen in my life, so I try so hard to push it away.

In the process of writing this book, I had to be reminded by a friend that I can be way harsh and hard on myself despite the fact that I forgave myself for my poor decisions. I had to move past how they made me feel because of my inability to not define my identity only on my actions! (Remember, we talked about this, to fully be real and love ourselves. I had to learn this the hard way.)

The judgment that I convict on me is always less than the grace I allow others. And my version of the truth is just that—my version.

I know that I will always fall short, but everyone will.

If I analyze more objectively, maybe I would not view myself as a promiscuous teen, but a depressed, confused, and angry young girl who was searching for a way to heal but didn't know how to start. And if I saw myself through the eyes of someone else, I would not judge her but love her instead.

So, I've come to realize, *even when you think nobody could possibly know you better than you know you, sometimes the image in the mirror can still be distorted, especially when you are really caught up in your feelings.*

Sin is sin, but only Jesus was without sin. There is redemption in recognition and turning to God for forgiveness and direction. **STOP the SELF-CONDEMNATION.**

"I have swept away your offenses like a cloud, your sins like the morning mist. Return to me, for I have redeemed you" (Isaiah 44:22).

Step back: Allow yourself the same grace you would offer

your best friend. Try to see things how they really are without the judgment, without the condemnation, and without the bias of your experience.

If you believe that all of your actions have consequences (and I agree they do), you still have to cut yourself a little slack.

For years, I blamed my post-pregnancy weight gain on that inappropriate behavior. I am shaking my head as I write this at the ridiculousness of the thought. A sliver of my brain was convinced that I was destined to remain overweight for the rest of my life as punishment for carnal sin when it was beautiful. (Pause for dramatic effect.)

I *know*, so crazy! Call it karma, or maybe I thought God knew that if I were to become fit and lovely again, I would be vain and/or even sinful. There are multiple issues with this thought process. While we do often suffer consequences related to our actions when they are out of line with God's will, especially when we sin, God does not hold grudges. He does not strike us with lightening or cancer or a semitruck as a result of that sin.

God does not punish us for the rest of our lives for a moment of sin.

Yes, we make mistakes, but God's grace says we are no longer condemned.

"There is therefore now no condemnation to them which are in Christ Jesus, who walk not after the flesh, but after the Spirit. For the law of the Spirit of life in Christ Jesus hath made me free from the law of sin and death" (Romans 8:1–2).

"He hath not dealt with us after our sins; nor rewarded us according to our iniquities. For as the heaven is high above the Earth, so great is His mercy toward them that fear Him. As far as the east is from the west, so far hath He removed our transgressions from us" (Psalm 103:10–12).

Also, you, me, we are in control of our own actions!

We may not be able to control what happens to us sometimes but we do control our actions and reactions.

We can't always control how we feel, but we can control what we do, and sometimes what we do can actually help how we feel.

We can wake up and be better today than we were yesterday.

I am not perfect. I am at minimum 40 pounds overweight as I write this. I am a workaholic who has a really hard time saying no and must really be diligent not to make myself so overwhelmed. I am so hard on myself. I have made bad decisions,

But I have done good things, too.

I am strong. I am smart. I am compassionate. I am loyal. I rose above that child who made poor choices. I received my bachelor's degree in three years, and I earned my doctorate despite my child having cancer. I got my masters just after having my third baby and working full time.

I am a leader and successful and I am not a perfect mom, but I am a good mom. I am a good person.

I lean on God. I look to him for direction and purpose. I talk to him. I desire to please him and learn about him. I share his grace and goodness with everyone who will listen. I have all of these abilities and attributes because of Him, my creator.

For a long time, I thought I strive to achieve because I want to be as different as possible from the small-town girl I was. But it's what I learned from her that makes me who I am today.

I thought that I owed it to God to do good things and big things because not everybody is blessed to live a full life.

I realize now I am a survivor and an achiever because I discovered the ability to rise by learning to lean on others and God and by looking inside of me and being honest about what I saw. **I am humbled by each accomplishment, not proud.** I once thought that having a child with cancer was the tragic event that changed who I became. But I now know that it took all of these experiences in my life, bad and good, to mold me into me.

For years I thought that maybe I could pretend that the experiences I buried were not a part of my life.

Now I know that they have allowed me to judge others less and show tolerance, to forgive others and forgive myself, to remind me to never be prideful and arrogant because I am by no means perfect, to not let anger rule my actions or my emotions, and to appreciate to its fullest the love and faithfulness of my husband and of God my creator.

I have only one chance to be me, to help others, to make a difference, to learn from my mistakes, and make the next day better. Each decision is a test. Each test failed is an opportunity to learn, and I am thankful for every day as a new opportunity.

I quote Joel Osteen to say, "You may be in the world, but you are not of the world."

We are able to rise above it, and we must believe that who we were created to be is more…more than our past sins, more than our circumstance, more than what others may say about us. God created you with purpose.

So…chin up. You can't rewind the clock. You can't uncry the tears once they fall. You *can* learn from your mistakes. You can forgive yourself. Show yourself some grace; **God does!** You can set goals. You control your actions, so you can do it!

You are beautifully and wonderfully made. You will not be perfect. **But character is formed in failure.**

"And he said unto me, My grace is sufficient for thee: my strength is made perfect in weakness…" (2 Corinthians 12:9).

You have endless flaws, just like me, and like a canyon etched by the river, you have unique asymmetry that has been defined by your experiences and growth followed by experience and growth. **The river moves and carries with it the past.**

Every day is a new chance to be better. A new chance to overcome and be strong because through God you are made new and because you control your actions. Every morning is a new opportunity to do good things because Ephesians 2:10 says we were created in Christ Jesus to do good works. We can live each day joyful because we are loved unconditionally by our Father, and we can find contentment because there is purpose in our life. We are blessed beyond measure in so many ways.

With that, my friend, know that you have the ability to live each day renewed and stronger with grit and a grateful heart. **And I truly hope you will!**

Running the Good Race

WHAT TRIUMPH LOOKS LIKE

"*Wherefore seeing we also are compassed about with so great a cloud of witnesses, let us lay aside every weight, and the sin which doth so easily beset us, and let us run with patience the race that is set before us, Looking unto Jesus the author and finisher of our faith; who for the joy that was set before Him endured the cross, despising the shame, and is set down at the right hand of the throne of God*" (Hebrews 12:1–3).

I was screaming so loudly my throat ached as the sound exited my body. I was in the middle of a crowd of people but had no fear of their judgment. I screamed because the excitement inside my chest could not be contained without the threat of explosion and because I hoped that my emotion on the wind could help push him through the finish line in first place.

The moment was surreal. We were in Athlone, Ireland. It was the very first stamp on my new passport, but this was no vacation.

It was an adorable quaint town filled with history and beauty on the River Shannon. But we were not here to sightsee.

It had only been a couple of years ago that Tyler was apprehensive about running track. He is quite competitive and his lack of confidence in himself on the track held him back from even trying. It was on a trip to the Endeavor Games in Oklahoma (a regional event for kids and adults with physical disabilities who can try a new sport, compete, and attempt to qualify to compete at the National Championships in track and field, swimming, and powerlifting) where he found his long lost love—the race.

I was attending the event due to a charity commitment. And since Tyler had been a few times several years before, he knew he would have friends there, and he never misses an opportunity to socialize!

I told him that if he were coming with me, he had to race. He wasn't really happy about this, but he knew I wasn't kidding, and it was a small trade-off to see his buddies. I wanted him to participate because I wanted to remind him that, win or lose, running alongside his friends and cheering each other on could still be fun. I also wanted to remind him that there was a time that running brought him joy, back before winning was important.

He brought home three gold medals that weekend. His face was lit up and his energy was high as we made the drive back from Oklahoma to Nashville. He loved getting to see his friends from all over the country that had disabilities similar to his own, but he was overflowing with the joy that racing gave him. The fact that he won compounded the excitement and gave him a renewed sense of confidence.

He knew that other meets, especially those at his high school, would bring more stiff competition, and that he would have to work hard, but he was determined that he was going to run and one day that he would be a Paralympian.

So, the work began. Tyler was fit but did not have the long, lean legs of many of the other runners. He is short in stature, like both me and his dad. He has Billy's muscular build. Tyler figured out quickly that it may take him more strides to get to the finish line than his opponents so he worked on making those strides as fast as they could possibly be and coming off the block like a bullet.

We were able to find him a team for the following year in the adaptive events (sports for those with physical differences like Tyler, in which you compete against those with similar challenges based on classification and age). He joined the track team at his high school and the local USATF club in Nashville. Track became a way of life. He watched videos of the fastest runners like Usain Bolt and Paralympic amputee gold medalists like Jonnie Peacock and Jarryd Wallace and began seeking to swallow every morsel of feedback from his coaches and senior athletes that he could. He listened and followed instructions. He was coachable and determined and practiced every day.

He didn't win first place in any of his high school meets that year, but he made it his goal not to come in last and throughout the season, his place at the finish line continued to improve. He went on to win several gold medals in regional adaptive events and even broke a record for the 100-meter dash at Junior Nationals.

When he received the email a few months later that he was chosen for the International Wheelchair and Amputee Sports Federation (IWAS) USA Team to represent our country for the 100-meter, 200-meter, and long jump in his classification, you can imagine the celebration in our household that night.

He was living a life determined. He was living a life devoted to God with a confidence in his own abilities because he believed God gave him strength and purpose. He knew firsthand that not everyone gets a chance to live. He was seeing the fruits of his labor, and he became encouraged to do more, work harder, aim higher. Along the way, he has encouraged others. He has continued to look to God for direction in his life, and he has stayed humble. He embraces positivity, and although he has struggles, he has peace.

In this moment on the sidelines, on Ireland ground, focused intently on this young man that I was so proud of and loved so much, I praised God. I was thankful because despite the struggles, Tyler would live life "on purpose," making the most of every second. He would win this race even if we didn't take home a gold medal.

The hard work boils down to a moment of truth. The 100-meter, his favorite event, lasts about 10 seconds. He came off the block like a powerhouse. His stride was flawless. Billy and I cheered at the top of our lungs, "*GO TYLER, GO TYLER, GO TYLER!*" as he whizzed passed us like a cheetah, fierce, and yet graceful.

This is what conquering adversity looks like.

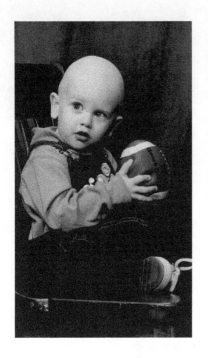 

Do you want more?

Go to www.thedrifteddrum.com website for more stories
about courage, compassion, and strength.

In Memory

Madelyn Beamon

Wesley McCall

Vivian "Abbi" Shaw

Shae Pierce

STAY CONNECTED

To learn more about The Drifted Drum Company, conquering adversity, and the business of encouragement, including access to other published works, Tyler Jones' exclusive apparel line, and author event booking, visit www.thedrifteddrum.com or connect with us on Facebook, Instagram, and YouTube.

 thedrifteddrum.com

 @thedrifteddrum
@dr.apriljones

 @thedrifteddrumco
@livebeautiful_dr.mom

 The Drifted Drum

 https://www.linkedin.com/in/
april-jones-pharmd-mba-25760757

CPSIA information can be obtained
at www.ICGtesting.com
Printed in the USA
LVHW110406070420
652429LV00001B/3